PRAYER ARMOR FOR DEFENSE

against the Enemy's Flaming Darts

REBECCA DAVIS

Pennycress Publishing

Contents

About this Prayer

Christians are in a cosmic battle.

Good against evil.

Light against darkness.

The forces of God against the forces of the wicked one.

In the lives of the abuse survivors I interact with, the battle is starkly evident to me. And though I do believe it's right to speak and act against evil, I know the ultimate solution in any spiritual battle is not to be found in speaking or acting.

The solution to the lies, schemes, and machinations of the enemy of our souls is to be found in the power of God in Christ alone, to be accessed by prayerful faith.

If we are to live successful and unshackled Christian lives and train our children to live free from Satan's attempts to control our minds, we must recognize the reality of spiritual warfare and rely upon the re-

sources provided by our risen Lord Jesus Christ.[1]

My own story

My blog, www.heresthejoy.com, gives a brief overview of how the Lord called me to work with abuse survivors from the church world (domestic, sexual, and spiritual), when I formerly hadn't even recognized that this phenomenon of "church abuse" existed. The majority of the work I do now involves meeting with abuse survivors one on one. (Much of my writing flows out of that more private work.)

As I've continued over the years to hear accounts of extreme abuse within the "Christian" context, I've continued to ask the Lord to increase my capacity. But still, because it seems that the human mind holds an almost limitless ability to execute horrors, my capacity continues sometimes to be exceeded.

---

[1] Fred Dickason, *Winning the War through Prayer,* WestBow Press 2016, Kindle loc. 265.

My thoughts can feel confused; I can feel overwhelmed and exhausted. I can be overcome by thoughts or feelings that distract me, turning me away from what's most important.

Then it becomes difficult for me to pray. But as it turns out, it is these times when I most need to pray.

At some point after I began to see that what was happening in my heart was actually a kind of spiritual battle, a friend recommended a short "spiritual warfare" prayer, and I began to pray it regularly. As time passed and I continued to mediate and pray and turn to God in times of great distress, I ended up writing my own, based on my understanding of who we are in Jesus Christ and the mighty work He has already accomplished.

I recognized the importance of working on writing my prayer during times of strength and peace, so that during times of overwhelm it would be ready for me . . . and I wouldn't find myself needing to pray when I could barely think.

So now I often reach for this prayer during those times. Often after I pray, I find that the confusion dissipates, the feelings of exhaustion and overwhelm quietly pass by, and the spiritual burden lifts.

It isn't the prayer, of course, that solves the problem. It is our mighty God, in the power of Jesus Christ, through the Holy Spirit.

But the prayer is designed to direct my thoughts and my cries to Him. As we look to Him, He has promised to strengthen our hearts.

Yes, fighting the devil, but . . .

You may think, the way I used to, "Why would the devil have anything to do with me? He's going to go after important people."

But this kind of thinking doesn't match with the many New Testament warnings to be on guard against the devil and his schemes.

And besides, the devil isn't all there is—he has his minions at work throughout the world to accomplish evil, as many foreign missionaries can attest, and as anyone who has been delivered from demonic influence can testify.

In many fundamentalist and conservative evangelical churches it seems that the sin in a sincere and seeking believer's heart is over-emphasized, while the attacks of the enemy go almost unmentioned. If the believer doesn't know how to distinguish, then these attacks can look like "thought sin" when they really aren't that at all.

When we as God's people are slogging through life trying to deal with our own hearts that we've been taught are deep wells of sin, this unrelenting inward focus will weaken us and draw our attention away from what is actually one of our most insidious enemies. How can we fight him if we don't even acknowledge that he's attacking?

If we neglect to fight *defensively* against the enemy, we'll find that ultimately our Spirit-empowered ability will be diminished to fight the *offensive* battles against evil that God has called us to fight. That is, the battles that need to be waged for the souls of others.

One day I hope to write more about offensive prayer as we go into the enemy's territory to rescue souls. But this is a defensive prayer, addressing the need for protection of our own souls and spirits, our own hearts, minds, and emotions, from enemy attack.[2]

Here it is for you

So I'm presenting it here, with hope that as you face your own battles, you'll be reminded that though we are at war and He has called us to fight, our Lord God of Hosts is ultimately victorious and He loves to bring strength, peace, and hope to the hearts of His own.

This is a prayer for you to use as an example or model, as you face your own battles. I hope you'll consider writing your own, to personalize it for yourself.

I'm praying for you.

---

[2] Throughout this book, I'll make references to teachings from the Word of God that I expand upon in my blog, Here's the Joy, which can be found at www.heresthejoy.com.

The Entire Prayer

Here is the Spiritual Armor Prayer in its entirety. In the following pages, I'll expand on it, with Scriptures.

The seven parts of the prayer go through seven stages:

1. You are my loving Savior, Lord.
2. I'm being attacked.
3. I want to repent and change in whatever way I need to.
4. I stand in Your strength alone.
5. You are protecting me and will deliver me.
6. Fill and strengthen me.
7. You are the ultimate Victor!

1. <u>Thanksgiving and truth</u>

Lord Jesus, thank You so much that You are my Savior every single day, every moment.

Every moment, You are my wisdom, righteousness, sanctification, and redemption.

Thank You that I can fully trust You because You are good and You are over all.

Thank You that You know me and You love me.

You are with me,

and by Your authority and Your Spirit You empower me to stand strong in You against the enemy.

2. <u>The attack against me</u>

Lord, today the deceiver of the whole world,

the one with the domain of darkness

who disguises himself as an angel of light

and seeks prey like a roaring lion,

wants to come against me through lies

that manifest in feelings and/or thoughts of overwhelm, despair, horror, pride, confusion, doubt, impatience, lust, irritability, self-condemnation, fear, distraction, self-focus, self-defense, self-exaltation, anger, weakness, exhaustion, anxiety, flesh-dependence, sadness, discouragement, or other such means of attack.[1]

3. Confession of sins

In any way I have given the devil a foothold,

have because of my desires been enticed and lured away from the faith,

have connected with these attractions and conceived and brought forth sin,

I confess and repent, asking Your forgiveness and cleansing from unrighteousness.

---

[1]This is my personal list. Your list will look different as you ask the Holy Spirit to reveal to you the workings of your own heart and mind.

4. Declaration of standing in Your Power

Through Your immeasurably great power, Lord Jesus Christ, only begotten Son of God, the same power manifest in Your Resurrection,

I resist the devil, standing firm against his schemes in the power of the Spirit, sober and watchful.

I ask You to rebuke the devil

and deliver me from evil.

I know that I fight with divine weapons,

and I expect to demolish strongholds through Your divine power,

because You came to undo the works of the devil.

5. Confidence in Your rescue

Because I stand in the righteousness of Jesus Christ alone, trusting in You,

because I desire to walk in the Spirit rather than in the flesh,

I know You will hear my cry for deliverance and will deliver me.

I know You will encompass me like a shield, with favor, with mercy, with songs and shouts of deliverance,

and with a great cloud of faithful witnesses.

6. Request for renewal

Renew me, O Lord, in Your strength, according to the power of the Resurrection.

Bring fresh awareness to my spiritual senses of the firm foundation of the solid rock under my feet.

Give me fresh awareness of your Living Water flowing in and through me.

Transform me and renew me with Your life and Your power.

Fill me with Your wisdom,

saturate me with Your fullness,

and cause me to abound with Your love.

7. <u>Further declaration of standing in Your Power</u>

I stand boldly by the blood of the Lamb,

and in the power of the Resurrection of the ascended and seated Christ, against the forces of evil.

I know that the devil and his minions have power,

but I also know that light is greater than darkness so that the darkness cannot put it out,

I know that those who are with me are more than those who are with them,

and I know that He that is in me is greater than he that is in the world.

PART ONE

Thanksgiving and Truth

Lord Jesus, thank You so much that You are my Savior every single day, every moment.

Every moment, You are my wisdom, righteousness, sanctification, and redemption.

Thank You that I can fully trust You because You are good and You are over all.

Thank You that You know me and You love me.

You are with me,

and by Your authority and Your Spirit You empower me to stand strong in You against the enemy.

*Lord Jesus, thank You so much
that You are my Savior
every single day, every moment.*

When the Bible speaks of Jesus as being the "Savior," it refers not only to a change of destination some sweet day when He takes me to heaven. It's also referring to a change of life **right now, today.**

His salvation is for the change of my heart's desires and my victory over sin right now.

Hebrews 7:24-25
but this man [Jesus],
because he continues forever,
has the intransmissible priesthood.
*Therefore **he is able also***
to save to the uttermost
those that come unto God by him,
seeing he ever lives
to make intercession for them.

The context of this Scripture that speaks of Jesus "ever living to make intercession for us"[1] shows that Jesus Christ's priesthood in the New Covenant is greater than that of the Old Covenant priests, in just about every way you could possibly imagine.

The resurrected life of Jesus Christ is endless, which means He is living and active and available for me today.

Amy Carmichael served God for many years as a missionary in India. But before that, as a twenty-something working with the low-wage young women of Belfast, she struggled to understand how she could live a holy life. She knew that all her ministry work wasn't going to make her holy. Struggling and striving to be good wasn't going to help her live a holy life. How could she do it?

---

[1] Does it feel unsettling to think "he ever lives to make intercession" for us, as if Jesus is standing in heaven holding His hands up and barely restraining God's wrath? Then you may find it helpful to read the blog post at www.heresthejoy.com: "Jesus as Intercessor: barely restraining God's wrath?"

Then one night at a conference, asking the Lord to show her, she heard a speaker pray, "Lord, we know that You are able to keep us from falling."[2]

Amy suddenly understood. Her ability to live a holy life didn't depend on her at all—it depended completely on the Lord Jesus Christ. Her part was to trust Him.

The same is true for each of us. He is our Rescuer in eternity. But He is also our Rescuer from sin and temptation *now*.

He wants to rescue us *today* in the middle of the spiritual battle we're undergoing *today*. Our part is to look to Him in faith.

---

[2] Jude 1:24-25.

Every moment, You are my wisdom,
righteousness, sanctification,
and redemption.

What are my wisdom, righteousness, sanctification, and redemption?

Are they to be found in the gospel? No, they are to be found in a *Person*, Jesus Christ.

Are they to be found in the cross? No, they are to be found in a *Person*, Jesus Christ.

He is my wisdom, righteousness, sanctification, and redemption.

1 Corinthians 1:30
But of him ye are reborn
in Christ Jesus,
who of God is made unto us wisdom
and righteousness and sanctification
and redemption.

This Scripture was written in the context of those who wrongly seek wisdom and power. The real wisdom and power come through

Jesus Christ alone. That way no one can boast, or be the rightful subject of flattery or praise from others.

I emphasize "every moment" because again, I don't want to relegate the application of the qualities of my Savior to my life in heaven. They apply to me *right now,* in my time of need.

There was a time in my life—before I began undertaking spiritual warfare for those who have been oppressed in the context of the church—when I was undergoing such intense spiritual attack, demonic attack, that I truly thought I was going to die. The Sunday morning that the attacks rose to their greatest intensity, I excused myself from church and drove home alone.

While I drove, I shouted. "Lord Jesus, YOU are all my righteousness! YOU are my only hope! YOU are all my salvation!"

By that time, after a year of the intense attacks, I knew the only way I would be delivered from the demonic onslaught that sought to pull me into the darkness . . . was Jesus Christ Himself. I called on His Name, directly and loudly. I put my faith in His Name alone, His Name, which represents the totality of all that He is for His people.

Righteousness, hope, salvation. And so much more.

As I called on the Name of the Lord Jesus, trusting in Him alone, without any striving of my own efforts, ultimately I found that He did deliver me.

*Thank You that I can fully trust You
because You are good
and You are over all.*

This can be a hard one if you feel like you're in the middle of darkness with no place to turn. It can be hard acknowledging that God is still good.

You may not be at a place where you can say this with your whole heart, because of massive betrayal by those who claim to be the people of God. But because it's true, if you speak it, you're still speaking truth instead of lies.

Psalm 5:11 (NKJV)
But let all those rejoice
who put their trust in You;
Let them ever shout for joy,
because You defend them;
Let those also who love Your name
Be joyful in You.

What does it mean, to love His Name? How will your life be different if you exalt the precious and beautiful and powerful Name of our Lord Jesus Christ, the Most High God?

When you lift up His Name, it will make a profound difference in your life.

This doesn't necessarily mean you'll see the difference immediately, but without a doubt you'll see it eventually. As you put your trust in the Lord, you can be confident that there will come a time that you will be filled with joy and your rejoicing will continue. You can count on it.

The demonic onslaught I described in the previous section ended that Sunday morning when I shouted my only hope in Jesus Christ. I wasn't sure it had ended for real, since in the past it had sometimes subsided for a bit but then returned. But after a month had gone by and the dark fog kept on lifting, I saw.[3] Then the Lord began to come very near and give me

---

[3] This experience is described more in the blog post "The thick darkness where God was," at www.heresthejoy.com.

a strong sense of His glory, His presence. For four months He swept away all my other responsibilities and allowed me to have the time I needed to bow in worship under the weight of that glory, as He showed me glimpses of Himself and His plan.

In the days and years that followed, I found that this glory experience strengthened me for the work He had called me to do.

As the Lord taught me about the truth of His loving presence and as I learned through prayer ministry to help myself and others experience the comfort and strength of His presence,[4] I saw the importance of simply understanding and appreciating this important truth.

We can fully trust Him because He is good and He is over all. Those of us who love His Name can trust He will bring us to a place of victory and joy.

---

[4] The prayer ministry I refer to is Immanuel Approach prayer ministry, more information about which can be found at www.immanuelsapproach.com and on video lectures from the founder, Dr. Karl Lehman.

*Thank You that
You know me and You love me.*

Jesus said in John 10:27,

*My sheep hear my voice,
and **I know them**, and they follow me*

John 10 is Jesus' beautiful "Good Shepherd" sermon. You, as His beloved sheep, will not only hear His voice, but will learn to distinguish His voice from the voices of others, as you spend time with Him and follow Him. An earlier verse (John 10:14) has said that His sheep know Him. But here it says that *He* knows *you*.

When you are His child, His knowledge of you isn't just to search out your sin so He can point at you a finger of condemnation. *It is knowledge of you as His precious lamb.*[5]

---

[5] If this seems hard to believe, the blog post "Thoughts for the Hopeless from Isaiah 40" at www.heresthejoy.com might help, as we believers in Jesus Christ learn to view ourselves in the way God views us.

"You know me, and you love me."

Ephesians 3:14,16-19
For this cause I [Paul] bow my knees
unto the Father
of our Lord Jesus Christ . . .
that he would grant you,
according to the riches of his glory,
to be strengthened with might
by his Spirit in the inner man,
that the Christ may dwell
in your hearts by faith,
that ye,
being rooted and grounded
in [love],
may be able to well comprehend
with all saints
what is the breadth and length
and depth and height
and to know the [love]
of the Christ,
which passes all knowledge,
that ye might be filled
with all the fullness of God.

Paul prayed this prayer for the Ephesian Christians. It's right and appropriate for us to pray this prayer for ourselves and all other believers.

God loves His people greatly, deeply, and profoundly, beyond explanation.

In the mountainous jungles of what is now called Papua, Indonesia, lived a boy named Siud. As the son of the witchdoctor, he had been charged with learning all the ways of the spirits. But Siud knew that the spirits his tribe sought to appease were spirits of fear and death.

One day he stood on a mountain looking out over the river. "There must be a Spirit who loves," he thought. "One day I'll find Him, and I'll follow Him." When Siud was grown, a missionary told him about the true God, who is so different from the lower spirits—not only is He powerful, *but He loves*. He loves! He loves not because He *has* to, but because He *wants* to. Siud trusted the true

God and became one of the leaders of the first Christian church of his tribe.

Our holy God wants all His children to know His love in an *experiential* way that far exceeds the intellectual knowledge of simply reading about it in a book and trying to hang on to it with your mind.[6] This experiential knowledge is to be accomplished by the power of His Spirit, through faith.

As your heart becomes open to Him, perhaps through the help of a prayer minister, He can *show* you His love. He can personally deliver His message of hope to you.

---

[6] If this feels like a difficult concept, you can continue to ask the Holy Spirit to open your eyes to His truth. Perhaps the blog post "Don't trust your feelings?" at www.heresthejoy.com will help.

You are with me

Matthew 28:20b
and, behold, I am with you always
even unto the end of the age.

Jesus said these words to the disciples who gathered around Him at the time of His Ascension, but He is always with His people.

To those who have experienced trauma, this truth "I am with you always" might not be comforting at first. But He can give an experiential awareness of this truth, of His great love and His loving presence, as described in Ephesians 3 in the previous section, that will bring this truth to a place of comfort.

Our Lord hates evil, but He does still allow it. He is willing, though, and more than willing, to gently come to the place of unhealed trauma wounds and bring deliverance, assurance, peace, and hope. In the lives of the people He has brought into my life, I've seen Him do that again and again.

and by Your authority and Your Spirit
You empower me
to stand strong in You
against the enemy.

Three wonderful New Covenant prayers that I return to over and over, as encouragement for myself and as a way to pray for others, are found in Ephesians 1, Ephesians 3, and Colossian 1.

In this prayer in Ephesians 1, the Lord shows us how we are to conduct spiritual warfare in our own lives.

Ephesians 1:17-21
that the God of our Lord Jesus Christ,
the Father of glory,
may give unto you
the spirit of wisdom and revelation
in the knowledge of him;
illuminating the eyes
of your understanding,
that ye may know

what is the hope of his calling
and what are the riches of the glory
of his inheritance in the saints
and what is
the exceeding greatness
of his power in us who believe,
by the operation of the power
of his strength,
which operated in the Christ,
raising him from the dead
and setting him at his own right hand
in the heavenly places,
far above all principality and power
and might and dominion
and every name that is named,
not only in this age,
but also in that which is to come

Through Jesus Christ, God has given power to His people to stand strong against all the attacks of the enemy. Through faith in Him we can appropriate all the power He has provided.

In this prayer in Ephesians 1, Paul describes the "exceeding greatness" of the power of God in those of us who believe in Jesus Christ. This power works by His strength, not by our own efforts.

Paul goes on to explain that this is the very same power, the very same, *that was at work in the raising of Christ from the dead.*

The very same power that raised Jesus Christ from the dead and set Him on high at the right hand of God the Father—that is the same power that is available to us.

That is the same power available to us.

Ephesians 3:20
Now unto him that is able
to do exceeding abundantly
above all that we ask or think,
according to the power
that works in us

Once again Paul emphasizes that our God is a God of great power, not the power of the flesh, but the power of the Holy Spirit. This power is not accessed by our own works, but by prayerful faith. We believe what He has said, and thus we trust Him to do His work in and through us. It is not of us, our works or schemes or plans, as the book of Galatians makes so very clear (perhaps especially Galatians chapter 3). It is through Him alone.

Ephesians 6:10
Finally, my brethren,
be strong in the Lord
and in the power of his might.

Ephesians 6:10 begins the "armor of God" passage. Though there's much to explore in these important verses, the emphasis here is the truth that we can be strong in the power of Jesus Christ, and the armor He gives us is promised to help us withstand the enemy's attacks.

For many years I lived my Christian life more or less this way: "I've got this, Lord. Thank you for giving me a brain and ability to work this out. I can handle this." It wasn't that

I didn't want God's help, it was more like I just wanted him close by in case, you know, the load I was lifting needed a second pair of arms.

Then came a time in my life when, because of an unusually challenging experience I had no rest in my soul and knew my mind was suffering. At that time I didn't know to name what I had experienced as trauma, and I didn't know what was happening, but what I did know was that I was in a desperate place, *unable to depend on myself at all in any way.* I had to cry out to the Lord for deliverance. Over the course of several days I struggled against the temptation to believe myself insane, hearing screaming voices in my head because of the experience I had just been through.

I felt as if the roaring lion was bearing down on me to devour me. I felt like Christian in *Pilgrim's Progress,* barely able to see Palace Beautiful, but needing to navigate the path between two—or two dozen—roaring lions before arriving there.

Over the course of those days instead of looking at those fearsome roaring lions, I looked to a different Lion: the Lion of Judah, crying out to Him again and again, standing on the truth of who He is again and again. When I came out the other side, it was with a greater strength and understanding of how to wage spiritual warfare, for both myself and others. It was with a greater understanding of my own utter inability and His excellent and all-sufficient ability to accomplish the work He has called me to do.

PART TWO

The Attack against Me

Lord Jesus, thank You so much that You are my Savior every single day, every moment.

Every moment, You are my wisdom, righteousness, sanctification, and redemption.

Thank You that I can fully trust You because You are good and You are over all.

Thank You that You know me and You love me.

You are with me,

and by Your authority and Your Spirit You empower me to stand strong in You against the enemy.

Lord, today the deceiver of the whole world,
the one with the domain of darkness
who disguises himself as an angel of light
and seeks prey like a roaring lion,
wants to come against me through lies
    that manifest in feelings and/or thoughts of overwhelm, despair, horror, pride, confusion, doubt, impatience, lust, irritability, self-condemnation, fear, distraction, self-focus, self-defense, self-exaltation, anger, weakness, exhaustion, anxiety, flesh-dependence, sadness, discouragement, or other such means of attack.

*Lord, today
the deceiver of the whole world,*

There are several names for Satan given in the Scriptures. This one is based on one in Revelation.

Revelation 12:9
And the great dragon was cast out,
the serpent of old,
who is called Devil and the Satan,
who deceives the whole world;
he was cast out into the earth,
and his angels
were cast out with him.

He is a deceiver—that's what he does. Some he deceives by convincing them there is no spirit realm and they should completely ignore him.

Others he deceives with promises of power or pleasure.

Some he deceives by convincing them they should focus on their own sin only and never try to understand the evil at work in the world.

Others he deceives with the illusion that he is overwhelming the world with his darkness, specifically our own cultures, which can draw us to despair or fear.

But he is real and he is at work.

And the power and pleasure will turn to dust.

And it is imperative that God's people understand the battle taking place in the spirit realm and in the world around them.

And he is ultimately a defeated foe.

We can cast aside his lies and walk in truth.

the one with
the domain of darkness

Colossians 1:12-13
giving thanks unto the Father,
who has made us worthy
to participate in the inheritance
of the saints in light,
who has delivered us from
the power [domain] of darkness,
and has translated us
into the kingdom of his dear Son,

The domain of darkness is ruled by the prince of darkness. His workers work their works in darkness rather than in light, because their deeds are evil (John 3:19).

But you, O child of God, you are not in the domain of darkness. From it you have been rescued forever. You are the child of your Rescuer, the King of Kings and Lord of Lords, along with every other one who has been rescued by the Great Rescuer. You are in the light, in the kingdom of His dear Son.

Even though we're now in the kingdom of the dear Son of God, though, the ruler of the domain of darkness continues to try to work his evil against those who follow their Shepherd. It is imperative for us to be on guard against him.

who disguises himself
as an angel of light

2 Corinthians 11:13-15
For these false apostles
are deceitful workers,
transforming themselves into
apostles of Christ.
And it is no marvel,
*for **Satan himself***
transforms himself
into an angel of light.
Therefore it is no great thing
if his ministers transform themselves
as ministers of righteousness,
whose end shall be
according to their works.

The deep truths of this passage of Scripture are worth meditating on, even though I doubt they would make it into many devotional books.

Paul couldn't have been more straightforward. Here he describes the false apostles that look very real and true and seem to be all about the glory of God and the gospel and righteousness, but they have "transformed themselves" (instead of being transformed by the power of the Holy Spirit) into something they are not, all the while still in actuality being *the ministers of Satan.*

Evil walks in our churches unrecognized by many. Some of us have had first-hand experience with such people.

Even Satan himself, the Adversary of our souls and of Christ's kingdom, transforms himself into an angel of light.

What does that look like? Well, it can look many different ways, but one thing is for sure, *it does not look like evil.*

Christians desperately need to walk in the power of the Holy Spirit to have the discernment we need, to look beyond the impressive presentation and to be willing to see, to hear, and to perceive the words and the works behind it. This is where the battle takes place.

and seeks prey like a roaring lion

I Peter 5:8
Be temperate and vigilant
*because your **adversary the devil,***
***as a roaring lion,** walks about,*
seeking whom he may devour

On the one hand, the Adversary will attract his prey like an angel of light, as the previous section describes. He can look really, really good. Attractive and beautiful, even to those who love God. Full of gracious words, full of talk about the glorious gospel and the awesomeness of Jesus.

On the other hand, even at the same time, this Adversary will seek out prey and try to devour them like a roaring lion, tearing them apart and spitting out the bones. His self-appointed mission is to steal, kill, and destroy.

This enemy of our souls finds willing human hands to assist in this evil work, even those who "transform themselves" as "apos-

tles of Christ" and "ministers of righteousness."

It is a very real and very intense battle
we're in, whether or not we want to
acknowledge it.

By the grace of God, He can open our spiritual eyes to the truth and give us alertness in
prayer to the workings of the enemy in our
churches. We can stand strong in prayer in the
righteousness of that other lion, the Lion of
the Tribe of Judah: our Lord Jesus Christ.

wants to come against me

Ephesians 6:12
For we wrestle not
against flesh and blood,
but against principalities,
against powers,
against the lords of this age,
rulers of this darkness,
against spiritual wickedness
in the heavens.

In Ephesians 6:10-11 Paul told the believers to stand firm in Christ and put on the armor of God. Now he tells the reason.

It isn't actually people who are our primary enemies, even though those "Christian" people who speak good words but whose lives speak something else are the most obvious evidences of the working of the Adversary. They are not our primary foe.

Rather, the primary wrestling match takes place in the spiritual realm, and, yes, even in our own souls, against the forces of evil. The forces coming against us from that "domain of darkness" consist of various spiritual authorities and powers, "rulers of this darkness."

We're told in the Scriptures that the battle is real. The fact that this battle is very little discussed in many evangelical circles doesn't for a moment diminish how real it is.

> *The Christian who knows little or nothing of a contest with spiritual foes is manifestly under the heel of his enemy, dwelling in an atmosphere of unreality and deception.*[1]

We ignore this battle to our peril, and to the peril of the desperate souls around us.

---

[1] Gordon Watt, *Effectual Fervent Prayer,* Great Commission, 1981, p. 21. (First published 1927.)

through lies

Here is the crux of the battle—the primary tactic of the enemy. Jesus said to the Pharisees

John 8:44
Ye are of your father the devil,
and the desires of your father
ye desire to do.
He was a murderer
from the beginning
and abode not in the truth
because there is no truth in him.
When he speaks a lie,
he speaks of his own,
for he is a liar and the father of it.

2 Corinthians 11:3
But I fear that
as the serpent deceived Eve
through his craftiness,
so your senses should be corrupted . . .
and ye should fall from the simplicity
that is in the Christ.

In the lives of the children of God who have trusted in Jesus Christ, the only tool Satan has to use against them is lies.

His lies can sound extremely convincing. *But they're not true.*

This is the lynchpin certainty to the battle in your own heart and mind.

You know the story about how circus trainers will train an elephant to stay put with just a small rope around the leg? They do it by starting the elephant with chains when he's young. By the time he's grown, he's so used to having those chains around his leg that a little rope will do the trick. He'll have no idea he could really get away.

Satan does the same thing, as the master of illusion. You have old thought patterns, old habits, old beliefs, and he wants to make you think you're still tied to them.

But you're not. In Christ you are free from those. When you truly see that truth, you'll see that you don't have to obey your old master. *You only have to see that Jesus Christ has rescued you and the devil no longer has pow-*

er over you. You can claim your true freedom in Christ and live according to that freedom.

You know evil people can come against you, of course. And there are those who have given themselves over to the Adversary and have allowed him further access. This was the case for the Pharisees (as Jesus described in John 8:44), who actively worked to accomplish the desires of the evil one, to further the kingdom of darkness, even while they pretended to be ministers of righteousness.

You may have had personal experience with those who speak lies that seem to come out of the deepest places of their character.

But as 2 Corinthians 11:3 indicates, even the children of the Kingdom of God can also unwittingly fall prey to the lies of the enemy. Smoke and mirrors. Deceit and trickery. Hypnosis and distraction.

In the heart of each individual child of God who has come to Him through Jesus Christ, we can rest assured that *the only weapon Satan has to harm our souls is lies.*

Some have taught that as soon as we learn about a weapon of Satan, we should simply recite with fervor Isaiah 54:17, *"No weapon formed against [me] shall prosper."*

This is a prime example of taking a Scripture out of context in order to use positive thinking to try to accomplish a goal.

Instead, the wisdom of Christ tells us to infuse our hearts and minds with the truth of Jesus Christ and His great salvation. In this way alone will Satan's lies fall as paper arrows against the shield of faith that covers our hearts. It is this way, as we have the mind of Christ, that the enemy's weapons of lies against us will not prosper.

*that manifest in feelings
and/or thoughts
of overwhelm, despair, horror, pride,
confusion, doubt, impatience, lust,
irritability, self-condemnation, fear,
distraction, self-focus, self-defense, self-
exaltation, anger, weakness,
exhaustion, anxiety, flesh-dependence,
sadness, discouragement,
or other such means of attack.*

I've noticed that the attacks against me almost always manifest first as *emotions*. So often, we're told to ignore our feelings, but that isn't healthy and isn't even Biblical—far from it. Feelings are not to be ignored—they are extremely important indicators of the state of my soul.

For me, some of the most common troubling emotions I experience are anxiety and overwhelm. Usually there are no words associated with these emotions—they're simply feelings, sometimes churning in my stomach.

The feelings and thoughts given in this section are simply my own personal list, developed over several years as I observed the ways the enemy attacked my mind and heart. As you ask the Lord to show you your own heart, you'll come up with a different list.

For example, irritability is sometimes one of my struggles, but you may never struggle with it. Loneliness or a sense of abandonment, on the other hand, isn't something I struggle with, but I know many people who do.

Notice that this list consists of definite sins (pride, impatience, etc.) as well as clear non-sins (overwhelm, sadness, etc.). I purposely didn't distinguish them, but simply wrote them down as they came to me. At this point I simply wanted to be aware of how the enemy attacks, whether it was through temptation to sin or by simply a strong emotion that could derail me.

When the feelings come, I have to stop and pray and think.

"Lord, what am I feeling and what's the basis for it?"

Sometimes the feeling might mean I need to take action in this physical realm; for example, one who lives in an unsafe home because of abuse of any kind might realize, "I feel anxious because my life and my children's lives have been threatened."

But often it's spiritual action that's called for, at least at first.

When it's a battle in the spiritual realm—like a matter of resisting temptation, or trusting God about a situation that He has assured me is in His hands, or staying stable and strong in the midst of a fight with evil—this is when Prayer Armor is most appropriate.

When I reach this part of the prayer, I ask the Lord to expose my heart to me. I'll then read through this list, the ways I know the enemy commonly attacks me, and I mentally circle the ones that resonate: yes, that one, that one, definitely that one. Sometimes in one prayer I might circle just a couple of the enemy's devices. Sometimes I might circle as many as ten.

Paul wrote to the Corinthians:

2 Corinthians 2:11
lest Satan should deceive us,
*for **we do not ignore his devices.***

I want to be fully aware of the designs, devices, and tricks Satan uses—in in my own life and in the lives of others.

1 Corinthians 14:33
For God is not
the God of disorder [confusion],
but of peace,
as in all the congregations
of the saints.

This is a Scripture I use especially when I'm being attacked by confusion—when my thoughts are a jumbled muddle.

The mind and heart of a Christian can be filled with confusion for a variety of reasons, not the least of which is years and years of spiritual abuse from a cult-like background, sometimes even spiritual abuse that facilitated sexual or domestic abuse.

In situations like this, getting help to untangle the confusion, through a wise friend or counselor or prayer minister can be essential. The enemy has clouded the thinking long-term, and the light of Christ will shine in bit by bit as we continue to look to Him.

But in situations in which the thoughts were clear but have become muddled, we can consider the possibility of an attack that can be faced with prayer armor.

When we think of "distractions," it seems that we often think of things like social media and entertainment. But for me, and for others I know, even researching into the wormhole of evil can sometimes become a distraction from what the Lord has called me to, and a way I seek to guard my heart.

As you spend time with the Lord and ask Him to show you your own heart, you'll see ways that your list pertains very particularly and uniquely to you.

PART THREE

Confession
of Sins

Lord Jesus, thank You so much that You are my Savior every single day, every moment.

Every moment, You are my wisdom, righteousness, sanctification, and redemption.

Thank You that I can fully trust You because You are good and You are over all.

Thank You that You know me and You love me. You are with me,

and by Your authority and Your Spirit You empower me to stand strong in You against the enemy.

Lord, today the deceiver of the whole world, the one with the domain of darkness who disguises himself as an angel of light and seeks prey like a roaring lion, wants to come against me through lies that manifest in feelings and/or thoughts of overwhelm, despair, horror, pride, confusion, doubt, impatience, lust, irritability, self-condemnation, fear, distraction, self-focus, self-defense, self-exaltation, anger, weakness, exhaustion, anxiety, flesh-dependence, sadness, discouragement, or other such means of attack.

In any way I have given the devil a foothold,

have because of my desires been enticed and lured away from the faith,

have connected with these attractions and conceived and brought forth sin,

I confess and repent, asking Your forgiveness and cleansing from unrighteousness.

In any way
I have given the devil a foothold

Now comes the part where I confess any sin the Lord has shown me. As I look over the list and see which things apply to me, some are obviously sins, but sometimes I'm not quite sure (confusion can increase that uncertainty).

But no matter what, my deepest heart wants to keep Satan from gaining a foothold in the "property" of my soul, which he can do through my sin, so I want to work through this part of the prayer.

Ephesians 4:26b-27
let not the sun go down
upon your wrath,
neither give place [a foothold]
to the devil.

The second half of Ephesians 4 speaks to God's people about putting off *"the old man who corrupts himself according to deceitful desires"* so that you can *"be renewed in the spirit of your understanding."* It then leads into the passage above.

That's what this is about—being aware of any way I may have given "place," or a foothold, to the devil, so that I can then through Christ have the victory in the spirit realm, where all the battles are ultimately fought.

About 15 or 20 years ago when I experienced a significant spiritual battle, I ultimately came to see it as something like the minions of Satan setting up camp in my backyard, while I was in my house, worried and scared, but not taking the necessary action to stand against them in the name of the Lord Jesus Christ, the only begotten Son of God.

There they were, having gained a "foothold," the practical outworking of which was a relentless battering-ram onslaught on my mind and heart. Even now, so many years later, I look back at that experience and say, "That was horrible."

But the Lord used that experience to inoculate me in a sense, giving me a keen desire to keep the workers of the enemy off the property that belongs to Him. That's the emphasis of this Scripture.

have because of my desires
been enticed
and lured away from the faith,
have connected with these attractions
and conceived
and brought forth sin,

James 1:14-15
But each one is tempted,
when they are **drawn away**
of their own lust [strong desires]
and enticed.
Then when lust has conceived,
it brings forth sin;
and sin, when it is finished,
brings forth death.

Here, then, is the anatomy of sin.

Each person is tempted when he (or she) is lured out and enticed *because of his own strong desire.*

This is the language of seduction, "lured out and enticed." Notice that the seduction isn't in itself sin—it's the temptation.

The enticing and being lured out is not in itself sin, but it happens because of something that connected with our desires.

If the process continues, though, then it leads to sin. When the strong desire has fully connected with the enticement, that's when sin takes place.

Some time ago when I was dealing with a situation that caused me sensations of over-whelm, despair, horror, confusion, anger, distraction, a sense of weakness, doubt, fear, exhaustion, sadness, anxiety, and discourage-ment (yes, it hit every single one of those), after the woman left my home I got out the ice cream and started eating it right out of the carton.

It wasn't the woman I was reacting to, but what had happened to her, the evil that had been perpetrated on her and the resulting grief and consequences.

But there I was with the ice cream, knowing full well that I should be going to the Lord.

Why did I go to ice cream instead of the Lord? This is the anatomy of sin—a small example to show a big problem.

A difficult situation caused me to be flooded with emotions. Within the context of those emotions, I believed lies. In this case the lies looked something like, "This is too difficult, God didn't take care of it then, and God's not taking care of it now. Ice cream. Ice cream will take care of it."

Of course those actual thoughts didn't go through my mind, and when I wrote them out just now, I saw how ludicrous they looked.

But the enemy offered the lies. I reached out and took them *because of my desires*.

Strong desire connects with lie.

Sin is birthed.

Stop it right there—confess and repent. Turn the other way!

Otherwise, the continued fornication between *strong desire* and *the lie* will bring about increased sin. When it is finished, it will lead to death.

Ephesians 4:22
But ye have not so learned of Christ,
if so be that ye have heard him
and have been taught by him,
as the truth is in Jesus,
that ye put off everything
concerning the old way of life,
that is,
the old man who corrupts himself
according to deceitful desires.

By faith turn to the only one who can deliver us from this path of death, Jesus Christ.

*I confess and repent,
asking Your forgiveness
and cleansing from unrighteousness.*

I John 1:9
If we confess our sins,
*he is faithful and just
to forgive us our sins
and to cleanse us
from all unrighteousness.*

Confession is stating the truth. How important it is to do that when there's any possibility I may have connected with a lie!

Repentance has come to be seen by many as simply consisting of tears and apologies. The honesty of the heart is judged by words and actions, which might or might not be pretended by a skilled actor.

Though tears and apologies might in some cases be appropriate, repentance would be far better defined along the lines of "coming to your senses," the way the prodigal son did

when he was in the pig sty, in the parable
Jesus told.

Luke 15:17-18
And when he [the prodigal son]
came to himself, *he said,*
How many hired servants
of my father's
have abundance of bread,
and I perish here with hunger!
I will arise and go to my father
and will say unto him,
Father, I have sinned against heaven
and before thee.

Picture him now, standing in the pig sty,
considering the life he has so profligately
wasted. He bemoans the husks the pigs are
eating, pondering his ravenous hunger.

Then, suddenly, he "comes to himself."

That's when he changed course. He deter-
mined to do something different, and he
began to set that new determination in motion.
Even though this "coming to himself" wasn't

accompanied by tears, still, that was his repentance. When the prodigal son returned home and spoke to his father, that was his expression of repentance. *But the actual repentance had taken place in the pigsty.*

Biblical repentance is a "change of mind" like that of the prodigal son, which says, "What was I thinking? Let me hurry up and get back where I belong! I was turning in the wrong direction, and I want to correct course."[1]

When we come to Him in confession and repentance, we can count on our Savior, our Rescuer, quickly and lovingly receiving us, cleansing us, restoring us, and setting us right again.

This is what He delights to do. Welcome home.

---

[1] For more on what repentance really is, these blog posts at www.heresthejoy.com might be helpful: "What does real repentance look like?" and "'Erring on the side of grace' when it comes to repentance?"

PART FOUR

Declaration of Standing in Your Power

Declaration of Standing in Your Power

Lord Jesus, thank You so much that You are my Savior every single day, every moment.

Every moment, You are my wisdom, righteousness, sanctification, and redemption.

Thank You that I can fully trust You because You are good and You are over all.

Thank You that You know me and You love me.

You are with me,

and by Your authority and Your Spirit You empower me to stand strong in You against the enemy.

Lord, today the deceiver of the whole world,
the one with the domain of darkness
who disguises himself as an angel of light
and seeks prey like a roaring lion,
wants to come against me through lies

that manifest in feelings and/or thoughts of overwhelm, despair, horror, pride, confusion, doubt, impatience, lust, irritability, self-condemnation, fear, distraction, self-focus, self-defense, self-exaltation, anger, weakness, exhaustion, anxiety, flesh-dependence, sadness, discouragement, or other such means of attack.

In any way I have given the devil a foothold,

have because of my desires been enticed and lured away from the faith,

have connected with these attractions and conceived and brought forth sin,

I confess and repent, asking Your forgiveness and cleansing from unrighteousness.

Through Your immeasurably great power, Lord Jesus Christ, only begotten Son of God, the same power manifest in Your Resurrection,

I resist the devil, standing firm against his schemes in the power of the Spirit, sober and watchful.

I ask You to rebuke the devil

and deliver me from evil.

I know that I fight with divine weapons,

and I expect to demolish strongholds through Your divine power,

because You came to undo the works of the devil.

*Through Your immeasurably
great power,
Lord Jesus Christ,
only begotten Son of God,
the same power manifest
in Your Resurrection,*

*Ephesians 1:18-19
illuminating the eyes
of your understanding,
that ye may know
what is the hope of his calling
and what are the riches of the glory
of his inheritance in the saints
**and what is the exceeding greatness
of his power in us who believe,**
by the operation of the power
of his strength*

This great power—I talked about it earlier in this prayer. But here it is again, because I needed to be reminded of it. This is the power that is the basis for our ability to accomplish what God calls us to do.

In her book *Counted Worthy*,[1] Isabel Anderson tells the story of José Pinzón of Colombia in the 1930s, who desperately wanted power and riches. Because Satanism promised power and riches, he studied it, with all its incantations and spells. But he found that he was only taken prisoner by dark forces, with terrifying fear of God's judgment.

Then, when he was desperate to be free from the dark forces, filled with fear, he met some joyful and fearless Christians who were handing out New Testaments.

As he read the New Testament, José saw that everything had been placed under the power of Jesus Christ, the head of the Church, and that the Church is His body. José wanted the riches of becoming part of the Church. He tried to do it through following rules, imitating the Christians by passing out Bibles, reading the Bible, and trying to live right.

---

[1] Isabel Anderson, *Counted Worthy,* Moody Press, 1964.

But he wasn't free. Finally he came to the place where the Holy Spirit showed him that the only way he could be free—and have the heavenly power and riches—was to believe in Jesus Christ, to fully put his trust in Him. He became a fearless witness for Him.

José found—as we can all find—that we can stand and move forward *in the power of the Resurrection of our Savior*—the same power that raised Him from the dead.

I resist the devil,
standing firm against his schemes
in the power of the Spirit,
sober and watchful.

James 4:7
Submit yourself, therefore, to God.
Resist the devil,
and he will flee from you.

In chapter 4 of his epistle, James talks about how the arrogant ones who look to themselves for help will be opposed by God. But the humble ones—the ones who look to Him for help—those are the ones He will empower by His Holy Spirit.

It is when *this* is our understanding—that we will indeed be empowered by the Holy Spirit as we look to Him for help—that we can then resist the devil and know that he will flee from us. We can be sure that the Lord will fight for us when we're humbly submitted to Him and looking to Him for help.

For someone as hard-headed as I've been through the years (with my "I think I've got this, God, but don't go too far away in case I need You" approach), it might take an extreme case of great desperation to come to this place of submission; yet when we rely only on Him to help us fight the assaults of the enemy, that's the very best place for us to be.

Ephesians 6:13
Therefore, take unto you
the whole armour of God,
*that ye may be able to **withstand***
in the evil day and stand fast,
all the work having been finished.

Having the whole armor of God is what enables us to *stand* in the evil day, to stand and continue to resist, rather than being laid flat by the attacks of the devil.

We put this armor on by faith, in the Spirit, trusting that Jesus Christ is all our armor, the Living Word of God who defeats the foe. He is the Living Word of God to fight against the enemy, and it is He to whom we lift our prayers. He is all our hope and the great Captain of our battle.

The person who has a faith in which the Lord Jesus Christ is not absolutely essential—the life and breath of that assurance—is one who has a defective faith. He is one who is building a house on the sand, as Matthew 7:26-27 describes, a house that will not withstand the winds and the storms of life.

I Peter 5:8-9
Be temperate and vigilant
because your adversary the devil,
as a roaring lion, walks about,
seeking whom he may devour.
Resist him steadfast in the faith,
knowing that the same afflictions
are to be accomplished
in the company of your brethren
that are in the world.

All the language of this passage in 1 Peter is the language of war, because we are soldiers who understand there is an ongoing battle and desire to be vigilant. Because of this, we remain temperate and watchful.

We resist the devil, who can attack at any time. We do this by remaining steadfast in the faith, and the faith with which we resist him is faith in the completeness of Jesus Christ to accomplish the victory for us.

This faith is what will keep the devil from devouring you. This is not faith that you "work up" in yourself, but faith that comes because you know our Lord is faithful.

This is what will keep this battle from becoming exhausting for you—it will become second nature to look to and cry out to Him.

I Thessalonians 5:6, 8
Therefore let us not sleep, as do others;
*but **let us watch and be sober.** . . .*
But let us, who are of the day,
***be sober**,*
putting on the breastplate
of faith and [love], and for a helmet,
the hope of [salvation].

I Peter 1:13
Therefore, having the loins
of your understanding
girded with temperance,
wait [patiently] in the grace
that is presented unto you
when Jesus, the Christ,
is manifested unto you

These Scriptures emphasize that we are warriors in a good work, fighting for truth and light, against the powers of darkness, through Christ.

Yes, we do need times of rest. But even then, and even when our own personal lives become peaceful, we are still warriors in a spiritual battle.

We must be sober; we must be watchful.

I ask You to rebuke the devil

Zechariah 3:2
*And the L*ORD *said unto Satan,*
The LORD **rebuke thee, O Satan;**
*even the L*ORD
that has chosen Jerusalem
rebuke thee;

Jude 1:9
Yet when Michael, the archangel,
contended with the devil,
disputing over the body of Moses,
he dared not bring against him
a curse of judgment, but said,
The Lord reprehend thee.

Both the Old Testament and the New Testament show the Lord as being the one to rebuke the devil, so this is why I ask the Lord to do the rebuking. However . . .

Some have said that because Christians have more authority in the spirit realm than the angels, which I do believe to be true, we can rebuke the devil ourselves. Is this correct? Perhaps, and you may want to write your prayer to reflect this. But I've written mine to reflect what the Scriptures emphasize, to the best of my ability.

No matter which way the prayer is written, though, it is a sure thing that the enemy of our souls needs to be rebuked. We can stand with confidence that he is ultimately a defeated foe.

and deliver me from evil.

Matthew 6:13
And **lead us not into temptation,
but deliver us from evil,**
*for thine is the kingdom
and the power and the glory forever.
Amen.*

Spiritual tests are not like school tests to see if I can get the answer right, but are more like the tests of refining that silver goes through when it is being rid of impurities.

The spiritual tests the Lord has taken me through have been turning points in my life and have without exception turned my heart more fully to the Lord.

But in every case, I needed to be delivered from evil.

And if I pray that I won't be led into situations that I'll see too late are simply traps of the devil, I'll find that I can live more consistently in the victory Jesus promises, rather than in the constant cycle I used to follow of sin-repent-try-harder-sin-repent-try-harder.

Again, this is a matter of faith.

I imagine Abraham coming into the land of Canaan, seeing those huge fortified cities and thinking, "*This* is the land God has promised *me?*" He was short on faith, even to the point that he would take someone who wasn't his wife to help him bear the son God had promised. (It didn't work.)

But after Isaac, the promised son, was born, Abraham lived 75 more years. This was 75 years we don't hear a lot about in the Bible, but it was 75 years of Abraham continuing to grow in his faith. By the end of it, his faith was so strong he was able to see to the end of the entire Old Covenant and look right to the New Covenant, which was the ultimate fulfillment of the Abrahamic Promise. He was looking, by then, for that Heavenly City, as Hebrews 11:8-10 tells us.

Of course that meant that all those huge fortified cities he saw around him (which he personally never inherited, by the way) he saw to be cities without foundation. He saw that only a city built and made by God would have a true foundation, because the only true foundation is an eternal one.

We can ask to be delivered from evil, because we are in the Kingdom of God, the Kingdom of the Father's dear Son (Colossians 1:13), and we know that this Kingdom is the only one of eternal value and importance. Unlike Abraham, who only saw the New Covenant but didn't receive it, we have actually received it, in Jesus Christ. We can "see to the end" of the physical things around us to know what's really important, as we're told at the end of Hebrews 11.

Then, with confidence we can ask the Lord to keep us safe from situations that will invite sin because of ignorance or pride. He can protect us from those.

We can also ask Him for deliverance from evil that others might tell us we must stay in "for our own good" or "to be obedient to authority."

Brother Yun, one of the founders of the Chinese house churches in the 1970s and 1980s, found himself often arrested by the Chinese government. But he also found that God wanted to deliver him from that evil through means of escape, again and again. One time he even escaped from prison after his legs had been broken, walking through several guarded gates.

We can ask our Lord and continue to keep asking Him to deliver us from evil, and be alert to any instructions He might give to us to get us out, which we trust Him to accomplish.

*I know that I fight
with divine weapons,*

Below is the great spiritual warfare passage of the Bible. It's important right here to read it in full, not just skimming over it, but reading it for two things:

First, recognizing the intensity of the spiritual battle we're in. Second, recognizing *how* we fight the battle.

Ephesians 6:10-18
Finally, my brethren,
be strong in the Lord
and in the power of his might.
Put on the whole armor of God
that ye may be able to stand firm
against the wiles of the devil.
For we wrestle not
against flesh and blood,
but against principalities,
against powers,
against the lords of this age,

rulers of this darkness,
against spiritual wickedness
in the heavens.

Therefore, take unto you
the whole armour of God,
that ye may be able to withstand
in the evil day and stand fast,
all the work having been finished.

Stand firm, therefore,
having your loins girt about
with truth
and having on
the breastplate of righteousness,
and your feet shod with the
preparation of the gospel of peace,
above all,
taking the shield of faith,
with which ye shall be able to quench
all the fiery darts of the wicked.
And take the helmet of salvation
and the sword of the Spirit,
which is the word of God;

*praying always with all prayer
and supplication in the Spirit
and watching in this
with all perseverance
and supplication
for all the saints.*

"So," someone once asked me, "how do I actually put on the armor of God? How do I go about it?"

It's all by faith, completely. But what you're putting on . . .

. . . is Jesus. He is all your protection and all your hope.

By faith I take to myself the salvation of my Lord Jesus Christ to cover my head.

By faith I take to myself the righteousness of Jesus Christ to cover my body.

By faith I take to myself the truth of the Lord Jesus Christ to cover my loins.

By faith I take to myself the peace-filled gospel of the Lord Jesus Christ, trusting Him to lead me as I walk forward.

By faith I take to myself the faith and faithfulness of the Lord Jesus Christ, as a shield to protect me from all the fiery darts of the enemy.

By faith I take to myself the *logos* of God—which is Jesus Christ Himself!—as a sword to help my fight all my battles in the power of the Spirit.

By faith I take prayer as a divine weapon, trusting my Lord Jesus Christ to accomplish His good purposes in me and through me.

I Thessalonians 5:8
But let us, who are of the day,
be sober,
putting on the breastplate
of faith and [love],
and for a helmet,
the hope of saving health
[the expectation of full deliverance].

Hope in the Scriptures is never a "maybe" thing the way it is nowadays. Hope in the Scriptures is always a *certainty*. Because of that, we can actually substitute for the word "hope" the word *expectation*, or even *anticipation*. Scriptural hope is a sure thing.

The Bible version I used translated the word "salvation" as "saving health."

This is full deliverance.

Picture our Lord Jesus delivering you from drowning in the ocean. In many modern-day teachings, His deliverance would be like leaving you on the beach to recover on your own and then get moving on your own to do what you're supposed to do . . . on your own.

But that isn't *full* deliverance from drowning. *Full* deliverance would be taking you to a place where you can recover, while He's right there beside you, feeding you what you need and tending you with balms and ointments. *Full* deliverance from drowning would include helping you get to a safe place and a full and productive life in the Spirit.

The salvation He offers is *full deliverance*. This is the expectation of *saving health*.

*and I expect to demolish strongholds
through Your divine power,*

*2 Corinthians 10:3-5
For though we walk in the flesh,
we do not war after the flesh
(For the weapons of our warfare
are not carnal,
but mighty through God
for the destruction of strong holds),
casting down reasonings
and every high thing that exalts itself
against the knowledge of God
and leading captive every thought
into the obedience of the Christ.*

Paul wrote 2 Corinthians partly to defend himself against the accusations of the Judaizers (men who claimed to be Christians but who wanted to bring Christians under the bondage of the law).

One of the accusations Paul had to fight was that he was doing what he did for self-serving motives and out his own fleshly strength. But in this passage he said, on the contrary, even though he did live in a physical body, the work he accomplished was not done by the strength of his flesh, but by the power of the Holy Spirit.

The same is true for us who fight spiritual battles the way God intended—the weapons we use aren't the physical ones, the ones that can be seen. Rather, the weapons we use are in the power of the Holy Spirit, *because this is a spiritual battle.*

The way we "cast down" the reasonings and imaginations in our own heart (and the way we pray for them to be cast down in the hearts of others) is by faith, not by works or our own fleshly effort. Then when our hearts are in line with the Spirit, we'll be able to move forward in the way God wants us to do.

In Paul's day the "fortresses" that needed to be cast down were the false teachings of the Judaizers, who sought to draw people into a pseudo-Christianity *based on a life of works rather than a life of faith.* This kind of false teaching could leave the door open for all kinds of evil. He knew how important was this struggle against "living by works" when he rebuked Peter for allowing even a foothold for it, described in Galatians 2.

Today the problems are often similar. Using the teachings of a pseudo-Christianity based on works rather than faith, many churches and parachurch organizations have been infiltrated by evil.

Just like David when he faced Goliath, when we're fortified against the attacks in our own hearts, we'll be far more prepared to face the enemy as he comes against us in the evil around us.

Sometimes there will be "physical" ways we go to battle, such as speaking or writing, as William Wilberforce did for the sake of slaves. But the preeminent weapons of our warfare will not be physical, but spiritual.

This means we will pray. We will seek God. We will listen to the Holy Spirit. We will move forward in faith step by step.

*because You came to undo
the works of the devil.*

This part of the prayer comes primarily from 1 John 3:8.

*For this purpose
the Son of God appeared,
that **he might**[2]
undo the works of the devil.*

Some translations of the Scriptures say here that Jesus came to "destroy" the works of the devil. But that Greek word that is translated "destroy" in some translations is actually translated "loose" or "untie" when the disciples brought the colt for Jesus to ride on through the city of Jerusalem.

The devil was active in the world during the days of the New Testament, and he is still

---

[2] The use of the word *might* here doesn't indicate "maybe." Rather, this part could be worded, "so that he could undo the works of the devil."

active. Jesus "undid" the devil's work by His sinless life, His substitutionary death, His triumphant Resurrection, and His ascension and seating in the heavenly places.[3] He did these things in order to accomplish our great salvation.

Now He is ready to rescue all those who come to Him by faith. And we can come to Him by faith again and again, many times a day, every day, as we look to Him for rescue in all of our life's circumstances.

Hebrews 2:14
Forasmuch then as the children
are partakers of flesh and blood,
he also himself likewise
took part of the same,
*that **through death***
he might destroy him
that had the empire of death,
that is, the devil

---

[3] For more on this great salvation, you can read "What kind of salvation did we get?" at www.heresthejoy.com.

In this Scripture, the "destroy" is not so much "crush" as it is "make ineffective." The same Greek word is used several times in the New Testament to show how the law is "ineffective" to bring salvation. It doesn't mean it, or he, has ceased to exist, only that it has ceased to be something or someone that must be followed and obeyed.

In the lives of those who come to Jesus Christ *and keep coming to Him* by faith in the power of the Spirit, He does make the works of the devil and the devil himself "ineffective" in accomplishing evil.

Jesus gave a foreshadowing of the rescue He would bring to many who were trapped in Satan's domain when He said in Mark 3:27,

No man can enter into
a strong man's house
and spoil his goods
except he will
first bind the strong man,
and then he will spoil his house.

Jesus, through His life, death, Resurrection, ascension, and seating, accomplished this "binding" and "spoiling" of the devil, who can certainly be a strong man in the souls of those who have not appropriated the life of Jesus Christ through faith.

And Paul, describing Jesus' triumph over sin, death, and hell, painted a picture of a Roman general in his triumphal march, with the captives trailing behind:

Colossians 2:15
and having spoiled
the principalities and the powers,
he made a show of them openly,
triumphing over them *in it.*

Satan now—as far as the one who belongs to Jesus Christ is concerned—is like a caged prisoner. He can call to you through his bars to try to pull you aside, but he can't get to you. He has no power to overcome you in his own strength, but only as you choose to come to the prison window, as it were, and listen to the lies he wants to whisper.

We don't need to obey him. We don't need to listen to his voice. We can choose instead to keep walking.

PART FIVE

Confidence in Your Rescue

Lord Jesus, thank You so much that You are my Savior every single day, every moment.

Every moment, You are my wisdom, righteousness, sanctification, and redemption.

Thank You that I can fully trust You because You are good and You are over all.

Thank You that You know me and You love me.

You are with me,

and by Your authority and Your Spirit You empower me to stand strong in You against the enemy.

Lord, today the deceiver of the whole world,

the one with the domain of darkness

who disguises himself as an angel of light

and seeks prey like a roaring lion,

wants to come against me through lies

that manifest in feelings and/or thoughts of overwhelm, despair, horror, pride, confusion, doubt, impatience, lust, irritability, self-condemnation, fear, distraction, self-focus, self-defense, self-exaltation, anger, weakness, exhaustion, anxiety, flesh-dependence, sadness, discouragement, or other such means of attack.

In any way I have given the devil a foothold,

have because of my desires been enticed and lured away from the faith,

have connected with these attractions and conceived and brought forth sin,

I confess and repent, asking Your forgiveness and cleansing from unrighteousness.

Through Your immeasurably great power, Lord Jesus Christ, only begotten Son of God, the same power manifest in Your Resurrection,

I resist the devil, standing firm against his schemes in the power of the Spirit, sober and watchful.

I ask You to rebuke the devil

and deliver me from evil.

I know that I fight with divine weapons,

and I expect to demolish strongholds through Your divine power,

because You came to undo the works of the devil.

Because I stand in the righteousness of Jesus Christ alone, trusting in You,

because I desire to walk in the Spirit rather than in the flesh,

I know You will hear my cry for deliverance and will deliver me.

I know You will encompass me like a shield, with favor, with mercy, with songs and shouts of deliverance,

and with a great cloud of faithful witnesses.

Because I stand
in the righteousness of Jesus Christ alone,
trusting in You,

It cannot possibly be overemphasized that the only righteousness we have—the only righteousness we have at all—is to be found in the righteousness of Jesus Christ. It is not found in our own works in any way at all.

Titus 3:5
not by works of righteousness
which we have done,
but according to his mercy
he saved us,
by the washing of regeneration
and renewing of the Holy Spirit.

This salvation Paul described here to Titus was the full salvation that encompasses not just our final destination but also our day-to-day lives.

The smile of God that we receive day by day comes from the mighty works that Jesus Christ has accomplished for us, and our faith in His works.

Romans 1:17
For in [Christ] is the righteousness of God revealed from faith to faith,
as it is written,
The just [or righteous]
shall live by faith.

We, the righteous, will live by faith. We need faith not only to change our eternal destination. We need it every day for our full salvation, what is commonly called our sanctification, which is accomplished by faith alone.

1 Corinthians 5:21
For he has made him to be sin for us,
who knew no sin,
*that **we might be made***
the righteousness of God in him

Romans 4:5-6
But to him that does not work,
but believes in him
that justifies the ungodly,
the faith is counted as righteousness.
Even as David also describes
the blessedness of the man
unto whom God attributes
righteousness without works

As these verses and all the New Testament indicate (as well as harbingers in the Old Testament), the righteousness of Jesus Christ is all our hope for all our salvation, *both justification and sanctification.* Even the life of practical holiness we want so much to live— even that is accomplished through faith alone.[1]

The story has been told of Marco Franco, one of the pioneer Christians in the nation of Colombia, in the 1930s. When he became a

---

[1] For more on this truth, you can read "Struggling with striving" at www.heresthejoy.com.

true child of God through the salvation of Jesus Christ, his former friends beat him until he was nearly dead. While Marco's body recovered, his mind and heart sank into blackness and despair, thinking dark thoughts against his attackers. "How can I even be a Christian if I think thoughts like these?" he wondered.

The man who had led him to Christ told him this was an attack from the enemy, Satan. "It is no sin to be tempted," he said. "It's a sin to welcome the temptation." Through trusting in Jesus Christ, Marco was delivered from his dark despair to a place of love and strength. He went on to win many of his fellow Colombians to the Lord.

When our eyes are opened to this glorious truth, when we stand in faith in Him, we can be confident that our Lord Jesus Christ will accomplish His good work in us and through us. We can expect and anticipate that we will see His good work in us as we continue to look to Him in faith.

because I desire to walk in the Spirit
rather than in the flesh,

Romans 8:3-4
For that which was impossible
to the law,
*in that it was **weak through the flesh**,*
God sending his own Son
in the likeness of sinful flesh
and for sin,
condemned sin in the flesh
so that the righteousness of the law
might be fulfilled in us
*who **walk not according to the flesh,***
but according to the Spirit.

Joy Ridderhof, founder of Gospel Record-ings, which recorded the gospel in little-known languages all over the world, found in the 1940s that her work was growing beyond the capacity of the workers to accomplish what they needed to do. "We need to take one day off every week for prayer," Joy said. The

113

workers, of course, resisted because they already weren't getting their work done. But after one year of *taking an entire day off every week for prayer*, they found they had accomplished more than they ever had before, and without the worry and stress.

My heart's desire—and that of every earnest Christian—is to walk according to the Spirit (energized by Holy Spirit energy, such as what Paul described in Ephesians 3:20), rather than by my own flesh (my own strength), to accomplish the work God wants to do in and through me.[2]

It is by faith that we are saved. It is by faith that we walk in the Spirit.

This will change not only our destination some sweet day. But today, now, moment by moment, it will change our desires, our delights, our duties, our direction, our determinations, our day-to-day, and our entire earthly destinies.

---

[2] For more about living according to the Spirit instead of the flesh you can see the post "Dear Christian, stop trying to die," at www.heresthejoy.com.

This understanding will enable us with the strength of the Lord as we stand firm against the enemy's flaming darts.

*I know You will hear my cry
for deliverance
and will deliver me.*

*Psalm 18:1-2
I will love thee, O Lord, my strength.
The Lord is my rock and my fortress,
and my deliverer;
my God, my strength,
in whom I will trust;
my [shield],
and the horn of my salvation,
and my high tower.*

I love how in Psalm 18 David starts with a declaration of determination. Not "help me to love You," but "I *will* love You." I love his proclamation of who God is to him—nine proclamations, in three sets of three—as the introduction to his story. My Rock, my Fortress, my Deliverer. My God, my Strength, the One in whom I trust. My Shield, the Horn of my salvation, and my High Tower.

Psalm 18:3
*I will call upon the L*ORD,
who is worthy to be praised,
so shall I be saved from my enemies.

I will call on the Lord, who is . . . who is what?

Not "who is very powerful."

Not "who is faithful." Even though those are both true.

But where is his focus? "Who is *worthy to be praised.*" Our Lord God of hosts is worthy to be praised because of His mighty works, His faithfulness, His great love, and for so many other reasons. David wraps it all up with this phrase.

Psalm 18:4-5
The pain of death compassed me,
and the rivers of Belial
made me afraid.
The pain of Sheol
compassed me about:
the snares of death came before me.

Yes, Lord, I feel overwhelmed by my enemies too, like David. They come upon me like floods. They ensnare me. They are too strong for me.

Psalm 18:6a
In my distress I called upon the Lord
and cried unto my God;

Yes, Lord, that's what I'm doing. I'm terribly distressed, and I'm crying out to You. You are the only one who can rescue me.

The whole psalm has me on the edge of my seat, but this next part (verses 6b-15) is especially exciting.

God heard.

God came.

And not quietly and calmly, but in a storm of thunder and lightning and hailstones and fire and blackness and earthquakes and storms and chariots.

With a blast of His breath, just like that, He vanquished the enemy.

Then . . .

Psalm 18:16-19
He sent from above, he took me,
he drew me out of many waters.
He delivered me
from my strong enemy,
and from those who hated me,
even though they were
too strong for me.
They were ready for me
in the day of my calamity,
but the Lord was my staff.
He brought me forth
into a wide place;
he delivered me
because he delighted in me.

Yes, Lord, I trust You. You will do that for me. I cry out to You to do that for me!

In the next section of Psalm 18 (verses 20-28) David makes one statement after another about his own integrity, his own righteousness in his own personal situation with Saul. For me, these are statements of my righteousness in Christ. So I can assert "I have kept the ways of the Lord, and have not wickedly departed from my God," because I know Jesus Christ had done that for me, and I am in Christ. I came to the Lord guilty, asking forgiveness, but now I stand before Him clean in the cleansing power of my Savior.

In the next section David's whole demeanor changes. He is no longer the fearful one, hiding in the shadows, but is a new man, fearless. The deliverance of the Lord has empowered him. He is strong.

Psalm 18:29
For with thee I have scattered armies;
and in my God
I have overcome walled defenses.

Yes, Lord, You will strengthen me to charge through theses enemies and overcome these walls.

O God of hosts, Your way is the perfect way. You are the only God. You are the only Rock. You give me hinds' feet to walk on my high places.

Show me my high places, Lord. I want to walk on those high places. Lord, increase my faith.

My arms are strong enough to break a bronze bow. Your gentleness has made me great. Now I have chased after my enemies and destroyed them, because you have filled me with strength.

One amazing statement after another in this psalm to meditate on, all pointing to the power and glory and mighty salvation of our matchless God. Through the salvation of my great Savior, I am victorious beyond my imaginings.

Therefore, the psalm closes, I will give thanks to thee, O Lord, in the midst of the people who do not know You. In their presence, I will sing praises to Your great Name.

And all of it, all of it, comes through the power of my Savior Jesus Christ. He, unlike any other, is worthy to be praised.

Psalm 18:30
As for God, his way is perfect:
the word of the Lord is precise:
a shield to all those that wait in him.

Psalm 18 reminds us that even when things are at their worst we can keep crying out to God to accomplish His good work. Don't give up.

I know You will encompass me
like a shield,
with favor, with mercy,
with songs and shouts of deliverance,

I could have made many observations about the implications of trusting in Jesus Christ and walking in the Spirit, but I wanted to focus on the "encompassing" aspect, because I'm in a spiritual battle, and in a battle our protection is of supreme importance.

Ephesians 6 tells us about the shield of faith, which is the encompassing of Jesus Christ all around us.

But the Psalms also speak about the encompassing for the righteous (not righteous in ourselves, of course, but righteous in Christ).

Psalm 5:12
For thou, LORD,
wilt bless the righteous;
with favour wilt thou compass him
as with a shield.

123

Psalm 32:10
There are many sorrows
for the wicked;
but he that waits in the LORD,
mercy shall compass him
round about.

Psalm 32:7
Thou art my hiding place;
thou shalt preserve me from trouble;
thou shalt compass me about
with songs [or shouts] of deliverance.

We are surrounded. Sometimes it may seem like we're completely surrounded by the enemy, and perhaps we are, outside.

But inside, ah, inside we're surrounded by the favor of God, the mercy of God, and our mighty God's songs and shouts of deliverance.

Russell Stendal, a 28-year-old missionary in the nation of Colombia, was kidnapped by revolutionaries there. But unlike Brother Yun (mentioned on page 91), the Lord told Russell to refrain from trying to escape and instead stay with his captors and give them the gospel. The Lord assured him that he would be protected for the work God had called him to do.

For five months, until his family raised the ransom money, Russell wrote, read the Bible aloud, argued theology, and discussed life with his captors, even while he had a rope around his neck. Because God was his shield and protector, he was not afraid.

Even in the midst of his enemies, some of whom fiercely hated him, Russell was shielded as he offered them the hope of redemption and rescue through Jesus Christ. Over the following years, hundreds of revolutionaries came to Christ.

O my soul, remember who wins this battle if we will only stand in faith, faith in His righteousness and power. In Him, through faith in Him, we are surrounded by His goodness and our souls are safe, no matter what storms are raging.

*and with a great cloud
of faithful witnesses.*

Hebrews 12:1
Therefore,
*seeing **we also are compassed about
with so great a cloud of witnesses,***
*leaving behind all the weight
of the sin which surrounds us,
let us run with patience the race
that is set before us,
with our eyes fixed on Jesus,
the author and finisher of our faith,
who having been offered joy,
endured the cross,
despising the shame
and was seated at the right hand
of the throne of God.*

In this great race, though our eyes will be fixed on Jesus, the one who accomplished the Great Work for us, still we're aware of the cloud of witnesses, those who have gone before us, who have trusted in Him.

Even as I learn more about evil people in positions of leadership and authority in the Christian world, still, I'm encouraged by the biographies of great God-followers in the Bible and biographies of notable Christians of history.

When we feel alone, we're not alone. There is a great host of other Christ-followers who have gone before us in history and who are following Him even now, in various places around the world. Some of them are obscure, little-known, but faithfully serving Him in their corner of the world. Sometimes those are the most inspiring to me.

We will keep our eyes fixed on Jesus, and we will remember that not only Bible heroes, but also many other Christians through the generations, have gone through similar trials. Their stories of faith in Jesus Christ, their expectation of His great work, and their focus

on the eternal perspective can encourage us
and renew our hope.

PART SIX

Request for Renewal

Lord Jesus, thank You so much that You are my Savior every single day, every moment.

Every moment, You are my wisdom, righteousness, sanctification, and redemption.

Thank You that I can fully trust You because You are good and You are over all.

Thank You that You know me and You love me.

You are with me,

and by Your authority and Your Spirit You empower me to stand strong in You against the enemy.

Lord, today the deceiver of the whole world,
the one with the domain of darkness
who disguises himself as an angel of light
and seeks prey like a roaring lion,
wants to come against me through lies
that manifest in feelings and/or thoughts of overwhelm, despair, horror, pride, confusion, doubt, impatience, lust, irritability, self-condemnation, fear, distraction, self-focus, self-defense, self-exaltation, anger, weakness, exhaustion, anxiety, flesh-dependence, sadness, discouragement, or other such means of attack.

In any way I have given the devil a foothold,

have because of my desires been enticed and lured away from the faith,

have connected with these attractions and conceived and brought forth sin,

I confess and repent, asking Your forgiveness and cleansing from unrighteousness.

Through Your immeasurably great power, Lord Jesus Christ, only begotten Son of God, the same power manifest in Your Resurrection,

I resist the devil, standing firm against his schemes in the power of the Spirit, sober and watchful.

I ask You to rebuke the devil

and deliver me from evil.

I know that I fight with divine weapons,

and I expect to demolish strongholds through Your divine power,

because You came to undo the works of the devil.

Because I stand in the righteousness of Jesus Christ alone, trusting in You,

because I desire to walk in the Spirit rather than in the flesh,

I know You will hear my cry for deliverance and will deliver me.

I know You will encompass me like a shield, with favor, with mercy, with songs and shouts of deliverance,

and with a great cloud of faithful witnesses.

Renew me, O Lord, in Your strength, according to the power of the Resurrection.

Bring fresh awareness to my spiritual senses of the firm foundation of the solid rock under my feet.

Give me fresh awareness of your Living Water flowing in and through me.

Transform me and renew me with Your life and Your power.

Fill me with Your wisdom,

saturate me with Your fullness,

and cause me to abound with Your love.

Renew me, O Lord, in Your strength,
according to
the power of the Resurrection.

Isaiah 40:31
but those that wait for the Lord
shall have new strength;
they shall mount up
with wings as eagles;
they shall run and not be weary;
and they shall walk, and not faint.

The strength our God has promised us was demonstrated in various ways throughout the miracles of the Bible. In the Old Testament, the Great Miracle that writers repeated over and over as the big example of God's mighty work was the deliverance from Egypt and the crossing of the Red Sea. God executed a mighty deliverance there (Psalm 78:12-16 is just one example).

But in the New Testament, that great miracle was no longer held up as the big example.

Instead, it was superseded by an even greater miracle, an even greater deliverance.

It is the great miracle of the Resurrection of Jesus Christ and the deliverance He accomplished for all His people through rising from the dead.

2 Corinthians 13:4
For though he [Jesus] was crucified
through weakness,
yet he lives by the power of God.
By which we also are weak in him,
but we shall live with him [even now!]
by the power of God in you.

What a shame that so many churches emphasize the cross but by comparison minimize the Resurrection.

The Resurrection is the most important event in history. Our deliverance wasn't fully accomplished until this Greatest of all Miracles was accomplished. The Resurrection was far more than simply our Savior Jesus defeating the power of death that the enemy had over Him so He could go back to heaven. It is every bit as much—*it is even more*—about His defeat over the power of sin the enemy wants to have over His children.

This, His dynamic power, is available to us as we seek Him, enjoy Him, live for Him, and fight our spiritual battles. As Ephesians chapters 1 and 3 emphasize, He offers that power to us, that very same power. It is available when we come to Him in faith and ask Him to bring down any hindrances in the lives of our spirits, for His work to be made manifest in and through us, for the glory that He wants to reveal through us.

Bring fresh awareness
to my spiritual senses
of the firm foundation
of the solid Rock under my feet

One of my desires is to regularly ask the Lord to renew or heighten my awareness of "things unseen," because the spiritual realm is eternal, while the physical realm is ephemeral.[1]

Psalm 34:8
O taste and see
that the LORD is good;
blessed is the man
that shall trust in him.

This is one of the Scriptures that make it clear we have spiritual senses. We live in a physical world where we can taste, see, hear, feel, and smell, but we also live in a spiritual

---

[1] The blog post "Ephemeral and everlasting" talks more about this, at www.heresthejoy.com.

world. God wants us and invites us to sense Him in that spiritual realm.

Even as we grow older and our physical senses may dim, our spiritual senses can become more greatly heightened. He delights to do that for us.

There are many aspects of who the Lord is and who I am that I need to know and experience with my spiritual senses. In this prayer, though, I emphasize *stability and safety*, primarily because the attacks of the enemy can throw me off balance.

And oh, there is so much to meditate on when it comes to the stability and safety of the Lord.

Psalm 18:2
The LORD is my rock and my fortress,
and my deliverer;
my God, my strength,
in whom I will trust; my buckler,
and the horn of my salvation,
and my high tower.

Psalm 40:1-3
*I waited patiently for the L*ORD*,*
and he inclined unto me
and heard my cry.
He brought me up also
out of the pit of hopelessness . . .
and set my feet upon a rock
and straightened my steps.
And he has put a new song
in my mouth,
even praise unto our God;
many shall see it and fear
*and shall wait on the L*ORD*.*

Psalm 62:1-2,5-7
Only in God does my soul rest;
from him comes my saving health.
He only is my rock
and my saving health;
he is my defence;
I shall not be greatly moved. . . .
My soul, rest thou only in God,
for my hope is from him.
He only is my rock

and my saving health;
he is my defence;
I shall not be moved.
In God is my saving health
and my glory;
the rock of my strength
and my refuge
is in God.

This is a sampling from the Psalms. David was well aware in his spiritual senses of the powerful upholding of the Rock of God under his feet.

What does it mean for our souls to rest in God?

I heard a story once that explained the difference between clinging faith and resting faith. The man spoke of a time he went on a horseback ride with cowboys, up a steep mountain at the edge of a cliff. As the sure-footed horses climbed the steep ridge, he watched the cowboys lean back in their saddles, enjoying the ride, enjoying the view for miles. But he gripped the saddle with his hands and legs, terrified, unable to look anywhere but at the narrow strip of ledge.

Finally one of the cowboys called back, "Trust your horse. He knows what he's doing. He's done this hundreds of times. You can just enjoy the view."

It took a while, but the man was finally able to relax his tight muscles, trust his horse, and enjoy the vast vista he could see for miles and miles. He could enjoy the crisp blue sky and the lazily circling hawks. He could trust his horse.[2]

Now, did he trust his horse before? Yes, he trusted him because he had no other choice. That was *clinging faith*. But when he trusted the horse fully, with a faith that said, "You've got this," that was *resting faith*.

When our lives our built on the solid Rock of Jesus Christ, we can rest our faith in Him, with confidence that He knows what He's

---

[2] John van Gelderen, *The Wind of the Spirit in Personal and Corporate Revival,* CLC Publications, 2012, pp. 84.

doing and He knows where He's going. He's got this.

Matthew 7:24-25
Therefore, whosoever
hears these words of mine
and does them,
I will liken him unto a prudent man,
who built his house upon the rock;
and the rain descended,
and the rivers came,
and the winds blew
and beat upon that house,
and it did not fall,
for it was founded upon a rock.

Jesus tells us that our lives are to be built on Him, in faith. Then He'll give us an awareness in our spiritual senses (where the battles take place) that He is strong and safe in the midst of the storms . . . and the attacks of the enemy. Even when the battle rages and the physical world around us crumbles, He will keep His people safe in their spirits.

> *Give me fresh awareness*
> *of your Living Water*
> *flowing in and through me.*

When you read the whole story of the Woman at the Well in John 4, you see that her spiritual thirst was awakened when Jesus spoke to her with these words:

John 4:13-14
Whosoever drinks of this water
shall thirst again,
but whosoever drinks of the water
that I shall give him shall never thirst,
*but **the water that I shall give him***
shall be in him a fountain of water
springing up into eternal life.

As you read that story, you can sense her thirst for that Living Water. She wanted it. And then she found that it could all be assuaged through Jesus Christ alone. As she stood in His presence and listened to Him, she knew. No wonder she wanted to tell everyone in her town about Him!

> *John 7:37-39a*
> *In the last day,*
> *that great day of the feast,*
> *Jesus stood and cried out, saying,*
> *If any man thirsts,*
> *let him come unto me and drink.*
> ***He that believes in me,***
> *as the scripture has said,*
> ***out of his [innermost being]***
> ***shall flow***
> ***rivers of living water.***
> *But this he spoke*
> *concerning the Spirit,*
> *which those that believe on him*
> *should receive*

Both of these Scriptures in John give an astounding truth for those who have put all their faith in Jesus Christ and look to Him alone for all their saving health: the river of God, the fountain of His waters, is not only flowing *to* us from God the Father, but is actually *flowing through us to others.*

When I meditate on this truth, I stand in amazement.

So when I pray, I ask that my spiritual senses be heightened, so that I can become more aware of the reality of this truth: by the power of His Spirit, He pours into me, so I never need to be thirsty. When I feel thirsty, He's right there.

The river is right there, in me.

Then through the power of His Spirit, as I trust Him, He causes the river of life to pour out of me to others, so they can drink too. What an incredible privilege.

We taste Thee, O Thou living Bread,
And long to feast upon Thee still;
We drink of Thee, the Fountain-head,
And thirst our souls from Thee to fill![3]

---

[3] From the hymn "Jesus, Thou Joy of Loving Hearts," by Bernard of Clairvaux and Ray Palmer.

Those who experience a taste, a sip of the true Jesus Christ, will long for more, long to be filled. And He has promised to provide.

Transform me and renew me,
with Your life and Your power.

Romans 12:2
And be not conformed to this age,
*but **be ye transformed**
by the renewing of your soul*
that ye may experience
what is that good and well pleasing
and perfect will of God.

How does the transforming come? By the renewing of our souls (or minds). What does that mean? How does this work out in practical application?

You may have been taught that this happens as you memorize Scripture and choose to think about good things, which can devolve into looking like just one more way for *you to make it happen by your own effort.*

But in truth, the transforming isn't something we can do ourselves. It happens only by the power of the Holy Spirit, as we trust in our Savior Jesus, looking to Him in faith.

What does this mean? How does this play out in real life? You can ask Him to show you how to live and walk in faith rather than formula.

As a young person, Joy Ridderhof, founder of Gospel Recordings (mentioned on pages 113-14) struggled greatly with worry and anxiety. But she learned to renew her mind by faith expressing her complete reliance on the Lord:

- **Praise** God in the midst of the trial, because He is up to something greater, even though I can't see what it is. (And the point is, I don't need to see it now.)
- **Trust** Him about it, and continue to trust Him.
- **Ask** Him to bring the trial to an end at the appropriate time for the sake of His Kingdom and His Name (being alert to what He wants me to do in that regard).

There was a time when I faced a significant trial in my own life and found myself overcome with worry. But at the same time I was studying the life of Joy Ridderhof. Like Joy, I purposed to turn my mind away from worry and fear and turn it to the Lord, being alert to what He wanted me to do. When I did, I found that He brought peace and inward deliverance. (He also eventually brought outward deliverance, but that seemed almost incidental to me in the lesson I needed to learn.)

This renewing of our minds that we cannot accomplish in our own strength is accomplished by the power of the Holy Spirit, through faith in Jesus Christ.

Titus 3:5
not by works of righteousness
which we have done,
but according to his mercy
he saved us,
by the washing of regeneration
and renewing of the Holy Spirit

2 Corinthians 4:16
Therefore we [faint] not;
but though our outward man
is wearing out,
yet the inward man is renewed
day by day.

Every day, even as we grow older, our inward self—our spirits—can grow stronger, by faith, as we continue to cling to the Lord and rest in the Lord, by faith.

This constant renewing, accomplished by the Holy Spirit as we trust in Jesus Christ moment by moment, day by day, is crucial in our lives. Without it, we won't be prepared to live the Christian life God has called us to. But with it, we'll find that we continue to gain spiritual strength in Him.

Colossians 3:10
and being clothed with the new man,
who is renewed in knowledge
according to the image
of the one that created him

Ephesians 4:22-24
that ye put off everything
concerning the old way of life,
that is, the old man
who corrupts himself
according to deceitful desires,
and be renewed in the spirit
of your understanding
and that ye put on the new man,
which is created in conformity to God
in righteousness
and in the holiness of the truth.

The renewal God commands in these Scriptures is so much more than trying to make moral effort to be good (which is ultimately impossible in the long run).

Instead, it is the renewing of the minds and souls that comes by faith in the power of the indwelling Christ. We express this faith and experience this power as we spend time focused on Him, learning from Him, and receiving the renewal He delights to impart.

Fill me with Your wisdom,

James 1:5
And if any of you lacks wisdom,
let him ask of God
(who gives abundantly to all,
and without reproach),
*and **it shall be given him.***

Everyone needs wisdom, especially those who are seeking to truly know God. As long as we're on this earth, we'll continue to need to be able to see life from His perspective, in all our life situations, as we seek to know Him better and enjoy Him more, and as we minister His love to others.

Even as we grow older and wiser, we'll continue to be thrust into circumstances that remind us how profoundly we need His wisdom. In His love, He never wants us to think "I'm good now. You can go help someone else."

There's something else to notice in James 1:5, something so encouraging. You can have a deep, settled assurance that He *wants* to provide wisdom for His children. He won't keep wisdom from you as you continue to look to Him, or give it only grudgingly.

So we continue to ask, desperately dependent on Him. And we continue to expect Him to be delighted to answer.

saturate me with Your fullness,

Ephesians 3:19
and to know the [agape love]
of the Christ,
which passes all knowledge,
that ye might be
filled with all the fullness of God.

When Paul prayed here that the Ephesians would be filled with the fullness of God, I used to picture being filled the way a cup is filled.

But that doesn't quite do this Greek word justice. A better understanding might be looking at being filled the way a sponge is filled, soaked up into every fiber. We might even use the word "saturated."

Now when I pray this prayer, I picture, in the spirit realm, my "self" not like a container to be poured into, but all my cells, to the tiniest part of each cell, with a longing for Him to saturate me with His Spirit.

When it comes to fighting the spiritual battles, we are helpless and hopeless without the strength of our Lord. But He delights to fill us up, to saturate us, with Himself.

---

and cause me to abound
with Your love.

One of the times I studied through Colossians, I paused on Colossians 1:4, thinking about how the Colossian Christians were filled with love, but I wasn't. I knew love was lacking in my life.

At that time, in 2000, I simply passively observed that sad characteristic in myself.

It wasn't until sometime later that I began to actually pray that *God would change my heart and fill me with His love.*

Philippians 1:9
And this I pray
that your [agape love] may abound
yet more and more
in knowledge and in all perception

As Paul prayed for the Philippians, I wanted my love to abound too, in a way that would be like Him. We want to love God, and we want to love others in the way that is most like God. This will mean our love for them will be demonstrated in the way that will help them the most.

For example, loving an abusive person *will not mean* passive acquiescence in allowing him or her to continue in his abuse. Even though that may seem to some like the only way to express love in such a situation, it is not loving, because this is encouraging him in a destructive path.

Rather, loving an abusive person will mean warning him about his sin, calling him to account for his abuse, and requiring that he bring forth "fruits of repentance" (Luke 3).

Love, the kind of love that is like Jesus, will recognize the serious nature of the spiritual battle and will recognize that some people give themselves over to evil. Love that is like Jesus will call out evil and expose the evil ones, while seeking to rescue and care for the ones who have been harmed.

Some people have given themselves over to evil ignorantly, never having heard of the real Jesus. This was the case with the Colombian revolutionaries who kidnaped Russell Stendal (mentioned on pages 124-25), and with many people groups that pioneer missionaries encounter. They need to be tenderly reached with the love of God.

Other people have given themselves over to evil having known and understood who the real God is and making a conscious decision to stand against Him and on the side of the evil one. Often these are the ones over whom God tells His people to pray destruction, in love for the ones they have harmed.

This is love that abounds in knowledge and in all perception. This love is our fuel for our spiritual battles.

PART SEVEN

Further Declaration of Standing in Your Power

Lord Jesus, thank You so much that You are my Savior every single day, every moment.

Every moment, You are my wisdom, righteousness, sanctification, and redemption.

Thank You that I can fully trust You because You are good and You are over all.

Thank You that You know me and You love me.

You are with me,

and by Your authority and Your Spirit You empower me to stand strong in You against the enemy.

Lord, today the deceiver of the whole world,
the one with the domain of darkness
who disguises himself as an angel of light
and seeks prey like a roaring lion,
wants to come against me through lies
that manifest in feelings and/or thoughts of overwhelm, despair, horror, pride, confusion, doubt, impatience, lust, irritability, self-condemnation, fear, distraction, self-focus, self-defense, self-exaltation, anger, weakness, exhaustion, anxiety, flesh-dependence, sadness, discouragement, or other such means of attack.

Further Declaration of Standing in Your Power

In any way I have given the devil a foothold,

have because of my desires been enticed and lured away from the faith,

have connected with these attractions and conceived and brought forth sin,

I confess and repent, asking Your forgiveness and cleansing from unrighteousness.

Through Your immeasurably great power, Lord Jesus Christ, only begotten Son of God, the same power manifest in Your Resurrection, I resist the devil, standing firm against his schemes in the power of the Spirit, sober and watchful.

I ask You to rebuke the devil

and deliver me from evil.

I know that I fight with divine weapons,

and I expect to demolish strongholds through Your divine power.

because You came to undo the works of the devil.

Further Declaration of Standing in Your Power

Because I stand in the righteousness of Jesus Christ alone, trusting in You,

because I desire to walk in the Spirit rather than in the flesh,

I know You will hear my cry for deliverance and will deliver me.

I know You will encompass me like a shield, with favor, with mercy, with songs and shouts of deliverance,

and with a great cloud of faithful witnesses.

Renew me, O Lord, in Your strength, according to the power of the Resurrection.

Bring fresh awareness to my spiritual senses of the firm foundation of the solid rock under my feet.

Give me fresh awareness of your Living Water flowing in and through me.

Transform me and renew me with Your life and Your power.

Fill me with Your wisdom,

saturate me with Your fullness,

and cause me to abound with Your love.

I stand boldly by the blood of the Lamb,

and in the power of the Resurrection of the ascended and seated Christ, against the forces of evil.

I know that the devil and his minions have power,

but I also know that light is greater than darkness so that the darkness cannot put it out,

I know that those who are with me are more than those who are with them,

and I know that He that is in me is greater than he that is in the world.

*I stand boldly
by the blood of the Lamb,*

*Revelation 12:10-11
And I heard a loud voice
saying in heaven,
Now is come salvation and virtue
and the kingdom of our God
and the power of his Christ;
for the accuser of our brethren
is cast down,
who accused them before our God
day and night.*
**And they have overcome him
by the blood of the Lamb**
*and by the word of their testimony;
and they loved not their lives
unto the death.*

There will be times of peace and calm in the battle. But even in the midst of the struggle, our spirits can be at rest, because all our righteousness is accomplished by Jesus Christ *and there are no hoops for us to jump through in order to be pleasing to God.*

But until the last day, described here in Revelation, the battle is still raging, the enemy still seeks souls to destroy, and we must still be on watch. He will destroy any way he can, and relentless accusation is often one of his most effective means.

And how is it that we can stand firm? It is only through faith in the power of Jesus Christ. In this case it is by faith in His sacrificial death for us, as the ultimate Lamb of God.

One of the earliest missionaries to the Muslims of Iran, in those days called Persia, was an Assyrian Christian, Pastor Yohannan. He arrived among the wild Kurds in 1879, hiring a young man to teach him the Kurdish language. This young man, Saeed, watched the pastor for weeks and months. He had known others who called themselves Christians and didn't at all practice what they preached. But this pastor was different. He demonstrated the love of God, again and again. When he prayed, thanking God for the blood of Jesus his salvation, he even prayed for his enemies, the Muslims. Saeed knew no Muslim would pray for his enemies. He had never known of a Christian to do that.

What Christian would do that?

Because of Yohannan's powerful testimony of love, Saeed eventually became the first Christian from the wild Kurdish tribe.

Yohannan was one of many who came into enemy territory, loving not his life to the death, confident in God's power to overcome the lies of the enemy by the blood of the Lamb and the word of his testimony.

*and in the power of the Resurrection
of the ascended and seated Christ,
against the forces of evil.*

In Ephesians 1:19-20 Paul prayed that the Ephesian Christians would know

*the exceeding greatness
of his power in us who believe,
by the operation of
**the power of his strength,
which operated in the Christ,
raising him from the dead***
*and setting him at his own right hand
in the heavenly places,*

*Ephesians 6:13
Therefore, take unto you
the whole armour of God,
that ye may be able to **withstand
in the evil day and stand fast,***
all the work having been finished.

When we *stand* and *withstand* in the evil day (which, in case you haven't noticed, is today), even as we pray a defensive prayer for ourselves, we are ultimately praying not only for ourselves, but for all who are and will be in the Kingdom of God. Then we'll find that we will graduate, maybe without even noticing, to *offensive* prayers—prayers that claim ground for Jesus and His Kingdom that the enemy has taken away.

The nation of Colombia was for decades known as a land of terrible violence, where the police and the military ruled like mobsters. But quietly, behind the scenes, the Spirit of God had also been working in that land for decades.

In 1996, a few Colombian Christians gathered and drove around the perimeter of the large, violently wicked, dangerous city of Cali, praying and praying for God to take that city for Himself.

They prayed not *defensive* prayer ("please protect and help me") but *offensive* prayer ("please deliver, rescue, and heal these lost souls").

Three years later, four hundred Colombian Christian pastors met to pray over a week of offensive prayer they were about to launch over Colombia, the largest prayer meeting the country had ever known. The pastors prepared with prayers of repentance and protection for themselves and each other.

That prayer meeting in a stadium began the next week with 3,000 Christians praying over their nation. Two nights later more than 35,000 Christians streamed into the stadium, filling it, with even more people standing outside waiting to come in and pray.

People in that stadium fell on their faces and wept. They wept over their own sins, the sins of their families, the sins of their city, and the sins of their nation.

They prayed for God to bring them a new day in Colombia, for the Spirit of God to sweep over their nation with His great salvation through Jesus Christ. And over the course of the coming years, some of the worst of the killers came to Jesus for salvation, and the Holy Spirit swept through the city.

From only 30 evangelical churches in the large city of Cali in 1980, the number of evangelical Christian congregations had burgeoned in 1990 to 250. By 2000 there were 700, and the number has been continuing to swell.

When we stand in the evil day, when we stand in "the day of small things," so much more is really going on behind the scenes, in the spiritual realm. We will trust that as we pray, God will work in the hearts of those He has called to Himself.

I know that the devil and his minions have power,

Colossians 2:15
and having spoiled
the principalities and the powers,
he made a show of them openly,
triumphing over them in it.

Ephesians 3:10
To the intent that now
unto the principalities and powers
in heavenly places
might be known by the congregation
the manifold wisdom of God,

1 Peter 3:22
who is at the right hand of God,
having ascended into heaven,
unto whom the angels
and the authorities and powers
are subject.

They wouldn't be called "powers" if they didn't have power.

In his seminal work *The Handbook for Spiritual Warfare*,[1] Ed Murphy tells of his introduction to the work of evil spiritual powers in the life of Christians. Like many Christians, he had firmly believed that Christians could not "have" a demon.

Everything changed for him when he found that his very own daughter, a girl who loved Jesus, was undeniably affected by demons. That experience caused him to re-examine his theology about the power and sphere of demons in the Word of God and to come to a new understanding of the Greek word that basically means "demonization."

It is true that the Word of God teaches that Satan's Kingdom has been defeated by the Lord Jesus Christ. It teaches that Satan and all his minions are subject to the Lord Jesus Christ.

---

[1] Ed Murphy, *The Handbook for Spiritual Warfare: Revised and Updated.* Thomas Nelson, 2003. pp. ix-xi.

But still, the Bible also teaches that these principalities and powers are active in the world, and have been even since the Resurrection. Though their powers are limited in the life of a believer, they can still exert influence and, if allowed in and left unnoticed, can cause havoc.

But I also know that light
is greater than darkness
so that the darkness cannot put it out,

John 1:1-5
In the beginning was the Word,
and the Word was with God,
and the Word was God. . . .
In him was life,
and the life was the light of men.
And the light shines in the darkness,
and the darkness apprehended it not.

Perhaps few examples of light overcoming darkness are more stunning than the stories of the work of the mighty Spirit of God in the Muslim world, as He has been bringing people to a knowledge of their sin and need for a Savior through many means, but most strikingly through dreams and visions that have consistently led them to seek out the first Christian they can find who can show them the way to Jesus.

No other country has been experiencing these phenomena more powerfully than Iran.

Taher was an exemplary Muslim in Iran. He took his faith so seriously that when first his daughter, then his wife, and then his son all converted to Christianity, he beat them severely and often and threatened to kill them if they didn't renounce the Christian faith.

God has different plans for different people, and His ways are higher than our ways. Some Christians in Muslim countries most certainly have given their lives for their faith.

But Taher's family were all able to escape into the night, with help from the Christians of their church.

In his grief, Taher looked to Allah, but found Jesus Christ. The light of Christ shone on him through a vision he had three times, the same each time. A man in radiant white came to him on a donkey. "I will cleanse you from your sins. I will give you rest. Believe on Me." Then another man asking him, "Do you know who that man was? That was Jesus Christ."

In spite of his strong belief in a way that led to darkness, Taher saw the light. He found the Christian church and believed on Jesus and became a changed man.

There are so many stories like this one throughout the world. We need to hear these stories. We need to be reminded that our God is one who loves to redeem those who are lost in darkness.

He loves to rescue His own children from darkness, when they cry out to Him, look to Him for deliverance, and listen to what He wants them to do.

*I know that those who are with me
are more than those who are with them,*

*2 Kings 6:15-16
And when the servant
of the man of God
was risen early to go forth,
behold, a host compassed the city
with both horsemen and chariots.
And his servant said unto him,
Alas, my master! What shall we do?
And [Elisha] answered,
Fear not;*
**for those that are with us are more
than those that are with them.**

For those of us dealing with demonized friends and loved ones, those of us who understand the extreme destruction that evil has worked in many organizations, including governments, churches, universities, military groups, the medical field, and law enforcement, the spiritual battle can seem so fierce and the power of evil so strong. We can feel like crying out, "Alas! What shall we do?"

Surely it has felt that same way to many people groups whose nations have been over-powered by evil government or church officials, overrun by the servants of those evil leaders.

Consider the Christians of Ethiopia whose land had been overtaken by communists, whose family members had been killed by the servants of that evil way.

But they knew, even still, that those who were with them were *more than* those that were with their oppressors.

In the late 1980s, Ekaso, an Ethiopian man who loved God, began walking to the top of his hill where he could see one of those com-munist prison camps. He knew the camp was evil and needed to go, but he also knew that there was absolutely nothing he could do in and of himself to destroy that camp.

But he knew God could. So he prayed and prayed, day after day. He prayed with anyone who would join him. "God! Destroy that camp!"

One day Ekaso prayed there with two other Christian men. Together they prayed all day.

The gigantic communist army camp had stood there for years. *Years*. But together the men, who had been praying for years, believed they should pray that God would destroy it *that very day*.

"Mighty God, show Your power!" they prayed. "Bring glory to Your Name by removing this evil thing!" They lifted their arms and turned the palms of their hands upward, pushing. "Push it out, O God!" they prayed.

Remember, these men had already been praying for years. Ekaso had been praying for years about this very communist camp that he still saw sitting there below him, unchanged.

They prayed all day, crying out to God to destroy the evil they saw before them. Late at night, past midnight, all three of them felt a whisper from the Holy Spirit of God that their prayer would indeed be answered that very day. They went home, praised the Lord, and slept soundly.

The next morning when they went to the top of the hill again, they saw that the army camp was empty. Little had they known, but according to the prayers of God's people, the communist government had been toppling, and the soldiers in that camp had been called away so quickly that they had left everything behind.

As soon as they were sure those ravaging soldiers were gone, the villagers began plundering the camp, taking whatever they needed to help them recover from all the devastation. In just a few hours, nothing was left of the huge army camp that had hung like a dark shadow of death over that valley for so long.

The power of God had overcome the powers of darkness. It had looked like only three old men with no weapons against a giant, well-equipped army. But the army of God was on the side of His people.

He still is. Let us pray.

*And I know that He that is in me
is greater than he that is in the world.*

*I John 4:4
Ye are of God, little children,
and have overcome them
because greater is he that is in you
than he that is in the world.*

There are books and speakers that will tell you the Christian life is accomplished by imitation. By striving. By developing habits.[2]

But that is not the Christian life described in the Bible. Jesus tells us that He is in us and He is our life (Colossians 3:4). This is how Paul could say in Philippians 1:21, "For to me to *live is Christ.*"

Sometimes young preachers will choose a famous preacher they want to imitate and proceed to study and copy his mannerisms,

---

[2] See, for example, *Godliness through Discipline*, by Jay Adams, father of nouthetic counseling. P&R Publishing, 1983.

his turn of a phrase, even his facial hair, because they want to have the success he has.

Let's say that the preacher they want to copy is not a secretly wicked hypocritical Pharisee, as some well-known ones are. Let's say he truly loves both God and others.

Copying the preacher will never give them the heartbeat of his life or his spiritual power. If all they want is to attract crowds and become famous, then they may well be able to do it by copying. But if they want to have the power of the Spirit of God, copying is not the answer.

If they seek to understand the heartbeat of a truly God-focused man's life, this will still only point them to Jesus, who does not expect us to "imitate" Him in the sense we think of the word, but to be indwelt by Him. He wants us to know Him experientially in His power, in the power of His Holy Spirit.

When we focus our hopes and desires on Him, He will show us what He can work within us. He can bring deliverance from the evil, bring healing into our lives, and give us the power to then go out and do battle for others against the forces of the enemy, who hates the God of heaven and counts eternal souls as objects to destroy.

Romans 8:37-39
Nevertheless, in all these things
we are more than conquerors
through him that loved us.
Therefore I am certain
that neither death nor life nor angels
nor principalities nor powers
nor things present
nor things to come
nor height nor depth
nor any creature
shall be able to separate us
from the [love] of God,
which is in Christ Jesus our Lord.

This is because we put all our faith in Him for our full deliverance.

I close with some words from George Mueller, a man who trusted God alone for the care of thousands of orphans, never asking anyone for money except the Lord Himself.

These words are not specifically about spiritual warfare, but are about faith, one of our primary weapons in the battle.

Some say, "Oh, I shall never have the gift of faith Mr. Mueller has got." This is a mistake – it is the greatest error – there is not a particle of truth in it.

My faith is the same kind of faith all of God's children have had. It is the same kind that Simon Peter had, and all Christians may obtain the like faith. . . . Their faith is precisely the faith I exercise, only, with regard to degree, mine may be more strongly exercised. Now, my beloved brothers and sisters, begin in a little way.[3]

One does not need to begin—nay, cannot begin—exercising faith by exercising *great* faith. But we can all start somewhere. We can all begin in a little way.

Perhaps we can start with faith that's willing to utter a short prayer that acknowledges the goodness and greatness of God, the attack we're experiencing, our desire for repentance and change, our confidence in His deliverance from the evil one, and our joy in His ultimate victory.

Let's begin.

My Prayer for You

I'm praying for you.

I pray that as you pray this prayer or another similar one that you write, you'll find that you experience increasing freedom from the attacks of the enemy.

I pray that your heart and mind will be filled with the knowledge of our Lord and Savior Jesus Christ, not only intellectual or "head knowledge," but deep, experiential, heart knowledge.

I pray that you will be filled with the empowerment, the energizing, of the Holy Spirit of Christ, to know Him fully and to long for the furtherance of His Kingdom in this world, and to have wisdom to know your place in accomplishing that great work.

I pray that you will be set free from the entanglements and burdens of sin, that your heart will beat with a love for God and others, and that your greatest desire will be to see other souls set free as well.

I pray that you will be free from the works-oriented gospel—which is not a gospel—that is preached so often in so many churches in these days. I pray that you will know real Christianity, the gracious outpouring of the Spirit of God manifest to others as the indwelling Christ maintains fulness of life.

I pray that you will know His indwelling as the rivers of living water springing out of you that He promised in John 7:37-39, so that other thirsty souls can drink, by the power of the Spirit.

I pray that in your life of love, you will long for the salvation of souls, the release of captives, the strengthening of the weak, the protection of the defenseless, the binding up of the wounded, and the healing of the brokenhearted.

I pray that you will come to know, in the deepest places of you heart, that *all of this is accomplished in Jesus Christ alone*.

I am praying for you.

Stories Referenced

The stories of missionaries and other exemplary Christians that I've referenced in this book have been taken from other books I've written:

With Two Hands: True Stories of God at Work in Ethiopia (Hidden Heroes #1), Christian Focus Publications, 2010.

Witness Men: True Stories of God at Work in Papua, Indonesia (Hidden Heroes #3), Christian Focus Publications, 2013.

Lights in a Dark Place: True Stories of God at Work in Colombia (Hidden Heroes #5), Christian Focus Publications, 2014.

Living Water in the Desert: True Stories of God at Work in Iran (Hidden Heroes #6), Christian Focus Publications, 2016.

Joy Ridderhof: Voice Catcher Around the Word (Potter's Wheel Books #2), Pennycress Publishing, 2015.

George Mueller: Pickpocket to Praying Provider (Potter's Wheel Books #3), Pennycress Publishing, 2015.

Brother Yun: The Heavenly Man of China (Potter's Wheel Books #4), Pennycress Publishing, 2017.

With Daring Faith: A Biography of Amy Carmichael, JourneyForth Books, 1987.

About the Author

Rebecca Davis has been a student of the Scriptures for about forty years, at first seeking to know "what God said," and later seeking to know God Himself. She is the author or collaborating author of several books about abuse in the Christian world (domestic, sexual, and spiritual), as well as several books of missionary stories, biographies, and devotionals for children.

Spending time listening to people's stories and offering hope through Jesus Christ is one of Rebecca's favorite pastimes. She has been married to her wise and good husband Tim for over thirty years, and together they have four children and two grandchildren. You can connect with her at www.heresthejoy.com.

About the Publisher

The pennycress is a small plant that grows wild, which has for generations been considered a lowly roadside weed, a nuisance.

Recent research, though, has shown that the pennycress is really a tiny powerhouse of energy that can be tapped and used as a renewable resource. So now instead of exterminating the weeds, farmers are buying seeds and planting acres of pennycress.

We love the picture of the lowly being lifted up. It reminds us of Mary in her song of praise to God, when she said, in Luke 1:48,52-53,

"for he has regarded the low estate
of his handmaiden;
for, behold, from now on all genera-
tions shall call me blessed.
He has put down the mighty

from their thrones
and exalted the humble.
He has filled the hungry
with good things,
and the rich he has sent empty away.

Even though Mary never saw that in her lifetime, she was so confident of it that she spoke of it as if it was in the past. And we're reminded, when we look at the lowly penny-cress, that those who are low will be exalted as they look to Him in faith. God speed the day.

About the Bible Version

For this little book, except as otherwise noted, I chose to use the Jubilee Bible, translated by Russell Stendal, a missionary to Colombia. As I wrote about Russell in *Lights in a Dark Place: True Stories of God at Work in Colombia*, I felt as if I got to know him.

In his "To the Reader" message at the beginning of this translation of the Bible, Russell explains his reasons for yet another translation, including the fact that the Spanish version he worked from had been translated by a man who had learned Hebrew as a living language rather than the dead one that later scholars studied. I have appreciated the fresh insights the version has brought to my own study of the Word of God.

Scripture Index

Made in the USA
Columbia, SC
15 October 2020

22882560R10109